Collins

Edexcel GCSE (9–1)
Maths

Grade 4–5 Booster Workbook

Greg Bryd

William Collins' dream of knowledge for all began with the publication of his first book in 1819. A self-educated mill worker, he not only enriched millions of lives, but also founded a flourishing publishing house. Today, staying true to this spirit, Collins books are packed with inspiration, innovation and practical expertise. They place you at the centre of a world of possibility and give you exactly what you need to explore it.

Collins. Freedom to teach

Published by Collins
An imprint of HarperCollins*Publishers*
The News Building
1 London Bridge Street
London SE1 9GF

Browse the complete Collins catalogue at
www.collins.co.uk

© HarperCollins*Publishers* Limited 2015

10 9 8 7 6 5 4 3

ISBN 978-0-00-811420-6

A catalogue record for this book is available from the British Library

The author Greg Bryd asserts his moral rights to be identified as the author of this work.

Commissioned by Lucy Rowland and Katie Sergeant
Project managed by Elektra Media Ltd
Copyedited by Joan Miller
Proofread by Joanna Shock
Answers checked by Amanda Dickson
Edited by Jennifer Yong
Typeset by Jouve India Private Limited
Illustrations by Ann Paganuzzi
Designed by Ken Vail Graphic Design
Cover design by We are Laura
Production by Rachel Weaver

Printed and bound by CPI Group (UK) Ltd, Croydon, CR0 4YY

Acknowledgements
The publishers gratefully acknowledge the permissions granted to reproduce copyright material in this book. Every effort has been made to contact the holders of copyright material, but if any have been inadvertently overlooked, the publisher will be pleased to make the necessary arrangements at the first opportunity.

The publishers would like to thank the following for permission to reproduce photographs in these pages:

Cover and title (top) sakkmesterke/Shutterstock.

Cover and title (bottom) Hulton Archive/Stringer/Getty Images.

Contents

Introduction

This workbook aims to help you succeed in GCSE Maths, Foundation tier. It gives you plenty of practice in the key topics in the main sections of your course. These sections are colour coded: **Number, Algebra, Ratio, Proportion and Rates of Change, Geometry and Measures, Probability and Statistics**. This book can be used as a stand alone revision aid to provide extra practice for Foundation level students, or can be used alongside Collins *Edexcel GCSE Maths 4th Edition Foundation Student Book*.

Question grades

You can tell the grade of each question or question part by the colour of its number:

Grade 3 questions are shown as blue

Grade 4 questions are shown as red

Grade 5 questions are shown as green

Use of calculators

Questions when you could use a calculator are marked with a ▦ icon.

Remember...

This reminds you about things which students often forget or get wrong.

Hint

A hint box is provided where extra guidance can save you time or help you out.

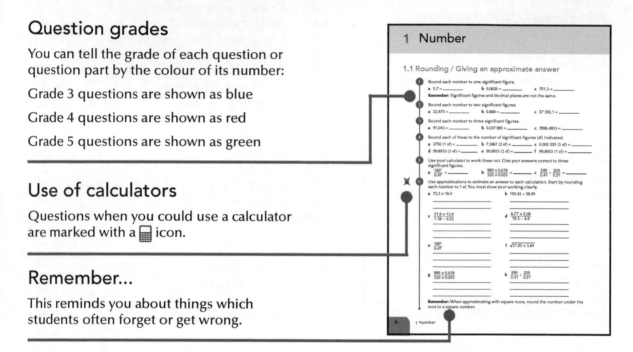

Revision papers

The revision papers help you to prepare for the exams. There are three papers, one to help you prepare for each exam paper. In the first revision paper you are not allowed to use a calculator (as in paper 1) and in the second and third you can use a calculator (as in papers 2 and 3).

Answers

Finally there are answers to all the questions at the back of the book. You can check your answers yourself or your teacher might tear them out and give them to you later to mark your work.

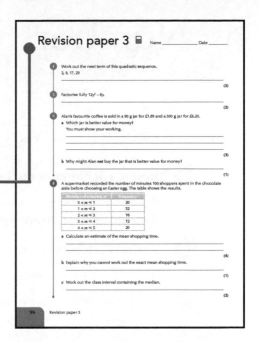

1 Number

1.1 Rounding / Giving an approximate answer

1 Round each number to one significant figure.

   a 5.7 = _____   **b** 0.0626 = _____   **c** 751.3 = _____

Remember: Significant figures and decimal places are not the same.

2 Round each number to two significant figures.

   a 22.475 = _____   **b** 0.868 = _____   **c** 57 392.1 = _____

3 Round each number to three significant figures.

   a 91.042 = _____   **b** 0.037 885 = _____   **c** 7896.4833 = _____

4 Round each of these to the number of significant figures (sf) indicated.

   a 3750 (1 sf) = _____   **b** 7.3861 (2 sf) = _____   **c** 0.005 555 (3 sf) = _____

   d 99.8933 (3 sf) = _____   **e** 99.8933 (2 sf) = _____   **f** 99.8933 (1 sf) = _____

5 Use your calculator to work these out. Give your answers correct to three significant figures.

   a $\dfrac{185^2}{0.47}$ = _____   **b** $\dfrac{989 \times 0.618}{320 \times 0.053}$ = _____   **c** $\dfrac{599}{0.41} + \dfrac{209}{0.51}$ = _____

6 Use approximations to estimate an answer to each calculation. Start by rounding each number to 1 sf. You must show your working clearly.

   a 72.3×18.4 **b** $193.42 \div 38.09$

   _____   _____

   _____   _____

   c $\dfrac{31.9 \times 13.9}{1.18 - 0.52}$ **d** $\dfrac{8.77 \times 5.08}{19.3 - 4.9}$

   _____   _____

   _____   _____

   _____   _____

   e $\dfrac{185^2}{0.47}$ **f** $\sqrt{21.93 \times 3.84}$

   _____   _____

   _____   _____

   _____   _____

   g $\dfrac{989 \times 0.618}{320 \times 0.053}$ **h** $\dfrac{599}{0.41} + \dfrac{209}{0.51}$

   _____   _____

   _____   _____

   _____   _____

Remember: When approximating with square roots, round the number under the root to a square number.

7 It took me 3 hours and 45 minutes to drive from Birmingham to Pembroke, a distance of 206 miles. My car travels 48 miles per gallon of diesel. The diesel cost £5.54 per gallon.

a Approximately how many miles did I travel each hour?

_____

b What was the approximate cost of the diesel for my journey to Pembroke and back again?

_____

_____

_____

1.2 Prime factors / Lowest common multiples / Highest common factors

1 a Write 28 as the product of its prime factors. Give your answer in index form.

_____

b Write 72 as the product of its prime factors. Give your answer in index form.

_____

2 Write down the lowest common multiple (LCM) of each pair of numbers.

a 5 and 7   b 28 and 72

_____   _____

3 Write down the highest common factor (HCF) of each pair of numbers.

a 12 and 20   b 28 and 72

_____   _____

4 Tariq coughs every two minutes.

Henry sneezes every five minutes.

Paul moans every eight minutes.

Tariq, Henry and Paul cough, sneeze and moan at the same time.

In how many minutes will they next cough, sneeze and moan together at the same time?

_____

5 Given that $A = 2^4 \times 3^3 \times 5^2$ and $B = 2^4 \times 3 \times 5^3$ write down, as a product of powers of prime factors:

a the highest common factor (HCF)   b the lowest common multiple
   of A and B (LCM) of A and B.

_____   _____

_____   _____

6 $11 \times 23 = 253$ $253^2 = 64\ 009$ $253^3 = 16\ 194\ 277$

a Write 64 009 as a product of prime factors in index form. _____

b Write 16 194 277 as a product of prime factors in index form. _____

c Write 253^7 as a product of prime factors in index form. _____

1.3 Indices ◩

1 Write each expression in power notation.

a $3 \times 3 \times 3 \times 3 \times 3 =$ _____

b $10 \times 10 \times 10 =$ _____

c $2 \times 2 \times 2 \times 2 \times 2 \times 2 =$ _____

2 Write each expression in power notation.

a $a \times a \times a \times a =$ _____

b $b \times b =$ _____

c $x \times x \times x \times x \times x \times x \times x \times x \times x \times x =$ _____

3 Simplify each expression. Write each answer as a number or letter to a single power.

a $5^2 \times 5^2 =$ _____

b $7^3 \times 7^5 =$ _____

c $2^{17} \times 2^3 =$ _____

d $3^9 \div 3^3 =$ _____

e $6^5 \div 6^4 =$ _____

f $8^{20} \div 8^{15} =$ _____

g $y^2 \times y^2 =$ _____

h $b^3 \times b^5 =$ _____

i $j^{17} \times j^3 =$ _____

j $m^6 \div m^2 =$ _____

k $a^9 \div a^8 =$ _____

l $t^4 \div t^4 =$ _____

m $\dfrac{7^6}{7^4} =$ _____

n $\dfrac{x^5}{x^2} =$ _____

o $\dfrac{x^2}{x^5} =$ _____

p $d^2 \times d^3 \times d^4 =$ _____

4 Simplify each expression fully.

a $2a^2 \times 2a^3 \times a^4 =$ _____

b $h^4 \times h^5 \div h^3 =$ _____

c $\dfrac{x^3 \times 3x^2}{x} =$ _____

d $\dfrac{b^2 \times 6b^3}{2b^4} =$ _____

e $\dfrac{4t^3 \times 3t^5}{6t^4 \times t} =$ _____

f $\dfrac{4a^4 \times 3a^3 \div 2a^2}{6 \times a^2} =$ _____

5 Given that $3^4 = x^2$ work out the value of x.

_____

1.4 Fractions ◩

1 Work these out. Give each answer in its simplest form and as a mixed number where appropriate.

a $\dfrac{3}{4} + \dfrac{1}{7} =$ _____

b $\dfrac{2}{5} + \dfrac{4}{9} =$ _____

c $\dfrac{5}{6} - \dfrac{3}{5} =$ _____

d $\dfrac{8}{9} - \dfrac{3}{4} =$ _____

2 Work these out. Give each answer in its simplest form and as a mixed number where appropriate.

a $3\frac{1}{3} + 1\frac{3}{5} =$ _____

b $\frac{3}{8} + \frac{3}{10} + \frac{4}{5} =$ _____

c $4\frac{1}{4} + 2\frac{2}{3} =$ _____

d $2\frac{2}{3} + 1\frac{3}{4} =$ _____

e $\frac{3}{4} \times \frac{1}{2} =$ _____

f $\frac{8}{9} \times \frac{3}{4} =$ _____

g $1\frac{3}{4} \times 2\frac{1}{2} =$ _____

h $2\frac{1}{2} \times 3\frac{1}{5} =$ _____

i $4 \times 2\frac{5}{8} =$ _____

j $8\frac{2}{5} \times 4 =$ _____

k $\frac{1}{4} \div \frac{1}{3} =$ _____

l $\frac{1}{3} \div \frac{1}{4} =$ _____

m $6\frac{2}{5} \times 1\frac{3}{5} =$ _____

n $1\frac{3}{5} \div 6\frac{2}{5} =$ _____

3 A patio is $3\frac{1}{4}$ m long and $2\frac{1}{5}$ m wide. What is the area of the patio?

_____

4 Amy's stride is four-fifths of a metre long. How many strides does she take to walk the length of a bus that is 12 m long?

_____

5 Work these out. Give each answer in its simplest form and as a mixed number where appropriate.

a $5\frac{1}{2} - \frac{5}{8} + 1\frac{3}{5} =$ _____

b $8 - 1\frac{3}{4} - \frac{7}{8} =$ _____

6 Work these out. Give each answer as a mixed number where possible.

a $2\frac{1}{5} \times 1\frac{2}{33} \times \frac{5}{7}$

b $\left(\frac{4}{5} \times \frac{4}{5} \right) \times \left(\frac{5}{8} \times \frac{5}{8} \right) \div \left(\frac{3}{8} \times \frac{3}{8} \right)$

_____

_____

_____

1.5 Percentage increase and decrease 🖩

1 Increase £250 by 12%.

_____

2 Increase £2.50 by 12%.

_____

3 Decrease 45 m by 12%.

_____

4 Decrease 4.5 m by 12%.

_____

5 Last year Xavier's salary was €21 550. This year it is €22 412.

What is the percentage increase of Xavier's salary?

_____

6 Hassan bought a van for £12 500. A year later he sold it for £8995.

Work out the percentage decrease in the value of the van.

_____

7 ABCD is a rectangle with length 35 cm and width 10 cm. The length of the rectangle is increased by 10%. The width of the rectangle is decreased by 10%.

```
A                    B
  ┌─────────────────┐
  │                 │ 10 cm
C └─────────────────┘ D
        35 cm
```

a What is the area of the new rectangle?

_____

_____

_____

b The new length is decreased by 10%. The new width is increased by 10%.

Without working it out, write down whether the area has increased or decreased. Explain how you know.

_____

8 The price of a flatscreen TV is usually £395 plus VAT (at 20%). It is on sale at 25% off this price.

What is the new price of the TV?

_____

_____

Remember: Do not simply take 5% off £395.

9 Give an exact answer when 4π is increased by 10%.

_____

1.6 One quantity as a percentage of another 🖩

1 In each case, express the first quantity as a percentage of the second.

a £5, £25 _____

b 8 kg, 32 kg _____

c 3.2 ml, 6 ml _____

d 12 minutes, 2 hours _____

e 375 g, 1 kg _____

f 2 hours, 1 day _____

2 Jodie scored 24 out of 40 in her English test. She scored 56 out of 90 in her history test. Use percentages to show that Jodie is better at history than English.

_____

_____

3 In the 2012 Olympic games, Great Britain entered 541 athletes. 279 of them were male. What percentage of the athletes who entered were female?

_____

4 In the 2012 Olympic games, Great Britain entered 541 athletes. 427 of them did not win a medal. What percentage of the athletes who entered did win a medal?

_____

5 A regular hexagon and a square both have a side length of 10 cm.

Give the perimeter of the hexagon as a percentage of the perimeter of the square.

_____

_____

6 Write 3×10^2 as a percentage of 5×10^4.

_____

7 Write sin 60° as a percentage of tan 60°.

_____

1.7 Compound interest 📧

1 Philippe has $2000 to invest. What does the calculation $\$2000 \times 1.05^3$ represent?

_____

2 Tebor invested £1000 in an account that pays 4.5% compound interest each year. How much will the account be worth after four years?

_____

3 The population of the Maldives was 390 000 at the start of 2009. The population growth rate is 5.6% each year. Estimate the size of the population at the start of 2015.

_____

4 A £20 000 car depreciates by 12% per year. How much is it worth after five years?

_____

_____

_____

_____

_____

5 In 2009, some experts thought there were as many as one million hedgehogs in the UK. Hedgehogs are now on the endangered species list as their numbers continue to fall by about 5% a year. How many hedgehogs are there likely to be in 2019?

_____

6 A certain type of conifer hedge grows at a rate of 15% each year for the first 18 years. Mr Jones buys a one-year-old plant that is 50 cm tall.

a How tall will it be in 15 years' time?   **b** How long will it take it to grow to 3 m?

_____   _____

_____   _____

_____   _____

7 Amy invests some money in stocks and shares. She makes 15% profit per year. How many years does it take for her to double her money?

_____

_____

8 Amy invests £2000 in stocks and shares. She makes an average profit of 6% per year for two years.

Ben invests £2000 in stocks and shares. He makes an average loss of 6% per year for two years.

How much more is Amy's investment worth than Ben's at the end of the two years?

_____

_____

_____

1.8 Basic powers and roots

 1 Complete this sequence of square numbers from 1^2 to 15^2.

1, 4, 9, _____

 2 Complete this sequence of cube numbers from 1^3 to 5^3.

1, 8, _____

3 Work these out without using a calculator.

   a $\sqrt{100} =$ _____   **b** $\sqrt{144} =$ _____   **c** $\sqrt[3]{64} =$ _____

   d $\sqrt[3]{1} =$ _____   **e** $\sqrt[3]{1000} =$ _____   **f** $\sqrt{49} + \sqrt[3]{125} =$ _____

   g $\sqrt[3]{5^2 + 4^2 - 3^2 - 2^2 - 1^2} =$ _____

4 Write down *both* square roots of 16. _____ and _____

5 Explain why −10 is one of the square roots of 100.

_____

6 Use your calculator to work these out. Give your answers correct to one decimal place.

   a $\sqrt{676} =$ _____   **b** $17.4^2 =$ _____

   c $\sqrt[3]{29.791} =$ _____   **d** $0.7^3 =$ _____

   e $\sqrt{0.04^3} =$ _____   **f** $\sqrt[3]{64^2} =$ _____

7 Work these out without using a calculator.

   a $\dfrac{\sqrt{13^2 - 5^2}}{2^3 - 2} =$ _____

   b $\dfrac{4^3 - 2^2}{\sqrt{5^3 - 5^2}} =$ _____

8 Given that $x = 2$ and $y = 5$, find the value of each expression, without using a calculator.

   a $x^2 + y^2 =$ _____

   b $y^3 - x^3 =$ _____

   c $\sqrt{y^2 + x^2 + y^2 - y} =$ _____

9 Work these out without using a calculator.

   a $\sqrt{0.49} =$ _____   **b** $\sqrt{1.21} =$ _____   **c** $\sqrt{0.04} =$ _____

Use your calculator to check.

1.9 Reciprocals

1 Work out the reciprocal of each integer, without using a calculator. Give each answer as:

   i a fraction   **ii** a decimal.

   a 2   **i** _____   **ii** _____   **b** 5   **i** _____   **ii** _____

   c 10   **i** _____   **ii** _____   **d** 100 **i** _____   **ii** _____

2 Look at your answers to question 1. What happens to the size of the decimal answers as the size of the integers gets bigger?

_____

3 Use your calculator to find the reciprocal of each decimal number.

   a 0.25 _____   **b** 2.5 _____   **c** 25.0 _____   **d** 0.025 _____

4 Without using a calculator, find the reciprocal of each fraction. Give your answers as mixed numbers where appropriate.

   a $\frac{7}{9}$ _____   **b** $1\frac{7}{9}$ _____   **c** $2\frac{7}{9}$ _____   **d** $3\frac{7}{9}$ _____

5 **a** What is the reciprocal of 0.4?   **b** What is the reciprocal of your answer to part **a**?

   _____   _____

   _____   _____

   c Multiply 0.4 by its reciprocal.   **d** Multiply 0.5 by its reciprocal.

   _____   _____

   _____   _____

   e Look at your answers to parts **c** and **d**. Does this always happen? Explain your answer.

   _____

   _____

6 Johan says that the reciprocal of a number is always smaller than the number. Give an example to show that Johan is wrong.

_____

7 Write down 8^{-1} in fractional form. _____

1.10 Standard index form

1 The Avogadro constant is 602 300 000 000 000 000 000 000.

Express this in standard index form.

_____

2 The total volume of seawater on Earth is about 1 370 000 000 000 000 000 m^3.

Express this in standard index form.

_____

3 A single cold virus is 0.000 000 02 m long.

Express this in standard index form.

_____

4 One atom of gold has a mass of 0.000 000 000 000 000 000 000 000 33 g.

Express this in standard index form.

_____

5 Write each standard form number as an ordinary number.

a $1 \times 10^4 =$ _____

b $1.2 \times 10^5 =$ _____

c $1.23 \times 10^{-5} =$ _____

d $1.234 \times 10^{-1} =$ _____

6 Work out each of these. Give all your answers in standard index form.

a $(6 \times 10^3) + (2 \times 10^2) =$ _____

b $(6 \times 10^3) - (2 \times 10^2) =$ _____

c $(6 \times 10^3) \times (2 \times 10^2) =$ _____

d $(6 \times 10^3) \div (2 \times 10^2) =$ _____

7 The speed of light is 300 000 km/s. Light takes $8\frac{1}{2}$ minutes to travel from the Sun to Earth. How far is the Sun from Earth, in kilometres? Express this distance in standard index form.

_____

_____

_____

8 You probably have about 2×10^{13} red corpuscles in your bloodstream. Each red corpuscle weighs about 0.000 000 000 1 g. Work out the total mass of your red corpuscles, in kilograms. Give your answer in standard index form.

_____

_____

_____

9 A factory produces 3.6×10^6 nails each year. Each nail has a mass of 5×10^{-3} kg. Of all nails produced, 0.75% are faulty. Work out the total mass of all the faulty nails produced in one year.

_____

_____

_____

1.11 Surds ✗

1   Write each expression as a single square root.

     a $\sqrt{3} \times \sqrt{5} = $ _____

     b $\sqrt{3} \times \sqrt{2} \times \sqrt{10} = $ _____

2   Work out the value of each expression.

     a $\sqrt{5} \times \sqrt{5} = $ _____

     b $\sqrt{3} \times \sqrt{2} \times \sqrt{6} = $ _____

     c $\sqrt{10} \times \sqrt{40} = $ _____

     d $\sqrt{6} \times \sqrt{2} \times \sqrt{12} = $ _____

     e $\sqrt{600} \div \sqrt{6} = $ _____

     f $\sqrt{63} \div \sqrt{7} = $ _____

3   Write out each expression in the form $a\sqrt{b}$ where b is a prime number.

     a $\sqrt{12} = $ _____

     b $\sqrt{80} = $ _____

4   Simplify each expression. Write your answer as a surd where necessary.

     a $2\sqrt{7} \times 3\sqrt{7} = $ _____

     b $3\sqrt{8} \times 2\sqrt{2} = $ _____

     c $4\sqrt{2} \times 2\sqrt{3} = $ _____

     d $3\sqrt{5} \times 2\sqrt{3} = $ _____

     e $3\sqrt{8} \times 3\sqrt{3} = $ _____

     f $\dfrac{4\sqrt{30}}{\sqrt{6}} = $ _____

     g $\dfrac{8\sqrt{125}}{2\sqrt{20}} = $ _____

     h $\sqrt{50} + 2\sqrt{32} = $ _____

     i $6\sqrt{12} - 3\sqrt{27} = $ _____

2 Algebra

2.1 Factorising

1 Factorise each expression.

a $6a + 12 = $ _____

b $4a + 8b = $ _____

c $4x + 6y = $ _____

d $8t - 6p = $ _____

e $2ab + 6ac = $ _____

f $5mn - 5mp = $ _____

g $p^2 + 5p = $ _____

h $7h - h^2 = $ _____

i $3x^2 + 2x = $ _____

2 Factorise each expression.

a $3t^2 - 3tp = $ _____

b $6x^2 + 9xy = $ _____

c $12a^2 - 8ab = $ _____

d $4b^2c + 8bc = $ _____

e $8abc - 6bed = $ _____

f $2ab + 4a^2b = $ _____

g $4x^2 + 6x + 8y = $ _____

h $6mp + 9bm + 3mt = $ _____

i $8cd^2 - 2cd - 4c^2d - 12c^2d^2 = $ _____

3 Write down an expression for the missing length in each rectangle.

a

Area = $8x + 6$ 2

?

length = _____

b

Area = $12 - 8p$ 4

?

length = _____

4 Write down an expression for the missing length in this rectangle.

Area = $t^2 + 4t$ t

?

length = _____

5 **a** Factorise $n^2 - n$. _____

b Given that n is a whole number, explain why $n^2 - n$ is always an even number.

_____

_____

6 Look at these shapes.

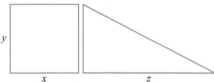

y x z

An expression for the total area of the square and the triangle is $xy + \frac{1}{2}zy$.

Factorise the expression for the total area of the square and the triangle.

_____

7 Factorise each expression.

a $x^2 + 3x + 2 =$ _____   **b** $x^2 + 6x + 9 =$ _____   **c** $x^2 + x - 6 =$ _____

8 Factorise each expression.

a $x^2 - 9 =$ _____   **b** $x^2 - 100 =$ _____

c $x^2 - 49 =$ _____   **d** $x^2 - 1 =$ _____

2.2 Brackets

Remember: Always be very careful with negative numbers.

1 Expand each expression.

a $5(a + 2) =$ _____   **b** $5(4 + x) =$ _____   **c** $5(x - y) =$ _____

d $x(x + 1) =$ _____   **e** $x(7 - x) =$ _____   **f** $x(x - y) =$ _____

g $5a(3 + a) =$ _____   **h** $5a(3a + b) =$ _____   **i** $5a^2(a - 3b) =$ _____

2 Expand and simplify each expression.

a $2(x - 3) + 3(x + 6) =$ _____

b $5(2x + y) + 4(2y + x) =$ _____

c $x(x + 3) + x(2x - 1) =$ _____

d $3x(x + 3) + 2x(2x - 1) =$ _____

e $4a(2a + 3b) - 3a(2a + 2b) =$ _____

f $3x(2x + 3y) + 2y(3y - 2x) =$ _____

g $5a(3a + 4) - 2a(3 - 4a) =$ _____

h $5p^2(2q^2 - 2r) + 2q^2(3p^2 - r) =$ _____

3 **a** Write an expression for the total area of the two rectangles. Use brackets.

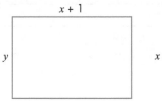 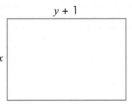

_____

b Expand and simplify your answer to part **a**.

_____

_____

4 Show that:

a $4(x + 1) + 6(x + 2) = 2(5x + 8)$ **b** $2(3x + 1) - 3(x - 4) = 3(x + 5) - 1$.

_____   _____

_____   _____

2.3 Solving linear equations

 Solve each equation.

a $4x - 3 = 5$ **b** $3 - 4x = 1$ **c** $\frac{x}{3} + 7 = 10$ **d** $2(3x + 1) = 32$

_____   _____   _____   _____

_____   _____   _____   _____

_____   _____   _____   _____

 Solve these equations.

a $\dfrac{12 - x}{3} = 5$ **b** $\dfrac{17 - x}{3} = 4.5$ **c** $\dfrac{20 - 2x}{4} = 3$

d $5x + 13 = 3(x + 5)$ **e** $2(1 - 5x) = 3(5x - 1)$

 Solve these equations.

a $5(2x - 3) = 2(x + 2) + 2(2x - 1) - 7$ **b** $3(2x - 1) + 4(x + 3) = 5(2x - 1) + 4(3x - 1)$

2.4 Solving quadratic equations

Solve each quadratic equation by factorising.

 $x^2 + 3x + 2 = 0$ $x^2 + 4x + 3 = 0$

 $x^2 + 6x + 9 = 0$ $x^2 - 6x + 9 = 0$

5 $x^2 + x - 6 = 0$

_____
_____
_____
_____

6 $x^2 - 2x - 8 = 0$

_____
_____
_____
_____

 7 $x^2 - 9 = 0$

_____
_____
_____
_____

8 $x^2 - 144 = 0$

_____
_____
_____
_____

2.5 Set up and solve linear equations

1 An isosceles triangle has angles of $2x°$, $2x°$ and $6x°$.

a Form an equation in terms of x. _____

b Solve your equation to work out the value of x. _____

c Give the sizes of the angles of the isosceles triangle. _____

2 Tom thought of a number. He divided it by two, and then added four. The result was one more than the number he first thought of.

a Use the above information to set up an equation. Use n to represent Tom's number.

b Solve your equation to work out the value of n.

_____
_____
_____

3 Nigethan drew two rectangles. They both had the same area.

5, $x - 2$, 3, $x + 4$

a Set up an equation in terms of x. _____

b Solve your equation to work out the value of x.

_____
_____
_____
_____
_____

4 Khalid is G years old. His son is 25 years younger than he is. The sum of their ages is 41.

How old is Khalid?

_____

_____

_____

_____

5 Kate is K years old. Her cousin is twice as old as she is. The sum of their ages is 36.

How old is Kate?

_____

_____

_____

_____

6 Paulo thought of a number. He multiplied his number by four. He added three to the result. He doubled that result and got 54.

What number did he start with?

_____

_____

_____

_____

7 Hammy uses a computer to draw a regular hexagon and a regular octagon, both with the same perimeter. The side length of the hexagon is $2x - 1$. The side length of the octagon is $x + 5$.

a Set up an equation in terms of x. _____

b Solve your equation to work out the value of x.

_____

_____

_____

_____

8 Abi draws a square of side length $10x$ cm. She then draws a triangle with side lengths of $16x + 2$ cm, $10x + 6$ cm and $4x - 2$ cm. The triangle and the square have the same perimeter. Find the value of x.

_____

_____

_____

_____

9 Lani starts with £21.50. Holly starts with £17.20. Lani buys five coloured phone covers and Holly buys three. The phone covers are all the same price. Lani and Holly both have the same amount of money left over. Work out the price of one of the phone covers.

_____

_____

_____

_____

2.6 Rearranging (changing the subject of) formulae

1 Rearrange each formula to make a the subject.

a $x = a + 6$ **b** $y = a - 6$ **c** $z = 6 - a$

_____   _____   _____

_____   _____   _____

2 Rearrange these formulae to make b the subject.

a $x = 4b + 6$ **b** $y = 5b - 3$ **c** $z = 6 - 2b$

_____   _____   _____

_____   _____   _____

3 Rearrange each formula. The subject is given in brackets.

a $V = IR$ (R) **b** $P = 2b + 2b$ (b) **c** $A = \dfrac{bh}{2}$ (b)

_____   _____   _____

_____   _____   _____

d $y = mx + c$ (c) **e** $y = mx + c$ (m) **f** $F = \dfrac{9C}{5} + 32$ (C)

_____   _____   _____

_____   _____   _____

4 Rearrange these formulae to make r the subject.

a $A = \pi r^2$ **b** $V = \pi r^2 h$ **c** $V = \dfrac{4\pi r^3}{3}$

_____   _____   _____

_____   _____   _____

_____   _____   _____

d $2r + 3r - 4 = 5$ **e** $P = \dfrac{1}{r}$ **f** $Q = \dfrac{2}{3r}$

_____   _____   _____

_____   _____   _____

_____   _____   _____

2.7 The nth term

1 Write down the name of each sequence.

 a 2, 4, 6, 8, … _____ **b** 1, 3, 5, 7, … _____

 c 1, 4, 9, 16, … _____ **d** 1, 1, 2, 3, 5, 8, … _____

2 The nth term of a sequence is $5n + 2$.

 a Write down the first four terms of the sequence. _____

 b Write down the 100th term of the sequence. _____

3 The nth term of a sequence is $\frac{1}{2}n(n + 1)$.

 a Write down the first four terms of the sequence. _____

 b Write down the 100th term of the sequence. _____

4 The nth term of a sequence is $n^2 + n$.

 a Write down the first four terms of the sequence. _____

 b Write down the 100th term of the sequence. _____

5 The nth term of a sequence is $2n^2 - n - 1$.

 a Write down the first four terms of the sequence. _____

 b Write down the 100th term of the sequence. _____

6 Work out the nth term of each sequence.

 a 5, 10, 15, 20, … _____ **b** 2, 4, 6, 8, … _____

 c 50, 100, 150, 200, … _____ **d** 20, 40, 60, 80, … _____

7 Work out the nth term of each sequence.

 a 6, 11, 16, 21, … _____ **b** 3, 5, 7, 9, … _____

 c 3, 7, 11, 15, … _____ **d** 1, 6, 11, 16, … _____

 e −4, −1, 2, 5, 8, … _____ **f** −80, −70, −60, −50, … _____

8 Work out the nth term of each sequence.

 a 10, 7, 4, 1, … _____ **b** 20, 16, 12, 8, … _____

 c 97, 87, 77, 67, … _____ **d** −5, −10, −15, −20, … _____

 e 0, −3, −6, −9, … _____ **f** 1, −9, −19, −29, … _____

9 Write down the nth term of each sequence.

 a $\frac{3}{4}, \frac{5}{9}, \frac{7}{14}, \frac{9}{19}, \ldots$ _____ **b** $\frac{1}{2}, \frac{2}{5}, \frac{3}{8}, \frac{4}{11}, \ldots$ _____

 c $\frac{3}{97}, \frac{7}{87}, \frac{11}{77}, \frac{15}{67}, \ldots$ _____ **d** $\frac{-1}{6}, \frac{-5}{7}, \frac{-9}{8}, \frac{-13}{9}, \ldots$ _____

10 Look at this sequence of circles.

  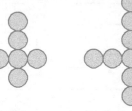 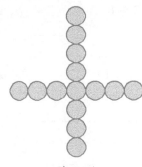

Shape 1   Shape 2   Shape 3   Shape 4

Write down the number of circles used in shape n. _____

11 A catering company uses tables in the shape of a trapezium. The diagrams show how many people can sit at different numbers of tables.

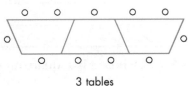

   1 table   2 tables   3 tables

a In this arrangement, how many people could sit at n tables? _____

b For a charity event, up to 150 people have to be seated. How many tables arranged like this do they need?

_____

_____

_____

_____

12 Write down the nth term of each sequence.

a 2, 4, 8, 16, 32, … _____   **b** 10, 100, 1000, 10 000, … _____

2.8 Inequalities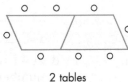

1 Solve each inequality.

a $x + 3 < 8$

b $x - 2 \geqslant 12$

c $x - 6 \leqslant 1$

d $3x + 5 < 17$

e $2x + 3 \geqslant 5$

f $5x - 2 \leqslant -12$

g $\frac{x}{5} > 6$

h $\frac{x}{2} + 1 \geqslant 5$

l $3(x + 4) < 6$

2 Write down the largest integer value of x that satisfies each inequality.

a $x + 3 \leq 8$

$x =$ _____

b $x - 2 < 12$

$x =$ _____

c $x + 7 < 3$

$x =$ _____

d $3x + 5 < 18$

$x =$ _____

e $3(x + 4) \leq -4$

$x =$ _____

f $5x - 3 < 12$

$x =$ _____

3 Write down the largest integer value of x that satisfies each inequality.

a $2x + 3 < 22$, where x is a positive, even number.

$x =$ _____

b $2x + 1 \leq 30$, where x is an odd number.

$x =$ _____

c $4x - 5 < 45$, where x is a square number.

$x =$ _____

d $2x - 1 \leq 24$, where x is a prime number.

$x =$ _____

4 Write down the inequality shown by each number line.

a

_____

b
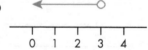

_____

c
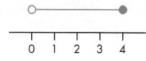

_____

d
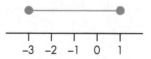

_____

5 **a** Which integers satisfy both inequalities in questions **4a** and **4b** above? _____

b Which integers satisfy both inequalities in questions **4b** and **4c** above? _____

c Which integers satisfy both inequalities in questions **4c** and **4d** above? _____

6 Draw each inequality on the number line.

a $x \geq 2$

b $x > 3$

c $x \leq 8$

d $2 \leq x \leq 4$

e $-3 < x < 0$

f $7 \leq x < 10$

7 Solve the inequality $2(4x + 3) \leq 18$ and illustrate its solution on the number line.

_____

_____

_____

8 Write down the inequality that represents the values of x that satisfy both of these inequalities.

$-2 \leq x \leq 4$ and $0 \leq x < 6$

_____

2.9 Real-life graphs

1 Farouk was travelling in his car to the airport. He set off from home at 10:00 am, and stopped on the way for a break. This distance–time graph illustrates his journey.

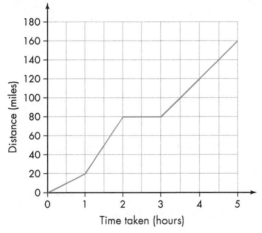

a At what time did Farouk:

  i stop for his break _____

  ii get to the airport? _____

b How far is the airport from Farouk's home? _____

c What was his average speed:

  i during the first hour _____

  ii during the last part of his journey? _____

2 Simon pours water into these containers at a steady rate.

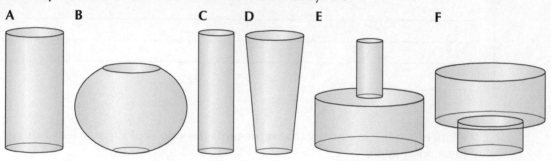

A   B   C   D   E   F

He measures the depth of the water in the containers over time and then draws these graphs.

1
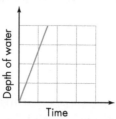

2
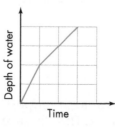

3

4

5
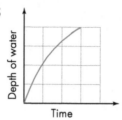

a Match the graphs to the containers. One container has no graph.

A = _____   B = _____   C = _____

D = _____   E = _____   F = _____

b One jar has not been matched. Sketch a graph for this jar.

Depth of water

Time

3 **a** Calculate the average speed during each stage of the journey shown on the graph.

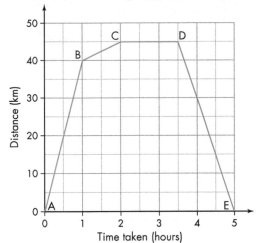

A to B = _____ km/h   B to C = _____ km/h

C to D = _____ km/h   D to E = _____ km/h

b How can you tell which part of the graph shows the greatest speed, just by looking at the graph?

_____

4 Work out the average speed of each of the journeys shown by these graphs.

a

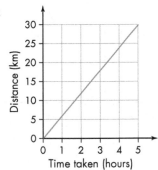

speed = _____ km/h

b

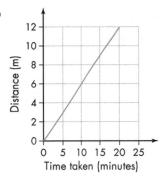

speed = _____ m/minute

c

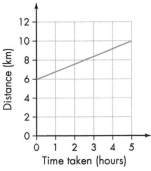

speed = _____ km/h

d

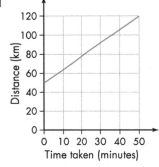

speed = _____ km/minute

5 The graph shows a race between Rob and Darren. Describe what happens in the race.

_____

_____

_____

_____

_____

_____

_____

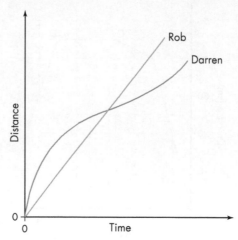

2.10 Gradient and intercept

1 Work out the gradient of each line, A to F.

A: _____

B: _____

C: _____

D: _____

E: _____

F: _____

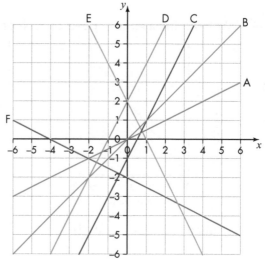

2 Write down the gradient of each line.

a $y = 4x + 3$ **b** $y = 3 + x$ **c** $y = -\dfrac{1}{2}x + 5$ **d** $y = 6 - 2x$

gradient = _____   gradient = _____   gradient = _____   gradient = _____

3 Write down the y-axis intercept of each line.

a $y = 3x + 4$ **b** $y = 3 + 2x$

intercept = _____   intercept = _____

4 Look at these equations of straight-line graphs.

A: $y = x + 2$ B: $y = 2x + 1$ C: $y = 2x + 2$ D: $y = 3x - 1$ E: $y = x$

F: $y = -x$ G: $3 - x = y$ H: $y = 3 - 2x$ I: $y = 4 - 2x$

a Write the letter of the line with the steepest gradient. _____

b Which pairs of lines are parallel to each other? _____

c Write the letter of the line that crosses the y-axis at the highest point. _____

5 Write down the equation of the line that:

a has a gradient of 1 and passes through the points (0, 1) and (3, 4) _____

b has a gradient of 2 and passes through the points (0, 3) and (2, 7) _____

c has a gradient of $\frac{1}{2}$ and passes through the points (8, 0) and (0, –4). _____

2.11 Drawing linear graphs

1 On the coordinate grid supplied, draw and label these lines.

a $x = 2$ **b** $x = -2$

c $y = -2$ **d** $y = 2$

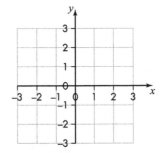

2 **a** Complete this table of values for $y = 2x - 1$ for $-2 \leqslant x \leqslant 2$.

x	–2	–1	0	1	2
y	–5			1	

b Draw the graph of $y = 2x - 1$ on the coordinate grid supplied.

c Use the graph to find the value of x when $y = 0$.

$x = $ _____

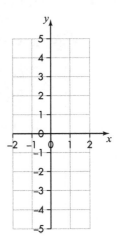

3 **a** Draw the graph of $y = 3x + 2$ for $-3 \leqslant x \leqslant 3$.

b Use the graph to find the value of x when $y = -4$.

$x = $ _____

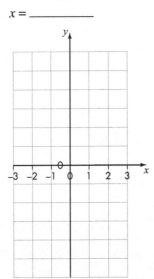

4 Use the gradient–intercept method to draw these graphs on the coordinate grid.

Remember: The gradient–intercept method means you start by plotting the intercept and then plot other points by using the gradient.

a $y = 2x + 2$

b $y = -\dfrac{1}{2}x + 2$

c $y = x + 2$

d $y = 5 - 2x$

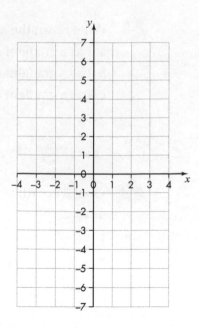

2.12 Drawing quadratic graphs 🔲

1 **a** Complete this table of values for $y = x^2 + 2$ for $-4 \leqslant x \leqslant 3$.

x	−4	−3	−2	−1	0	1	2	3
y	18	11				3	6	

b Draw the graph of $y = x^2 + 2$ on the coordinate grid below.

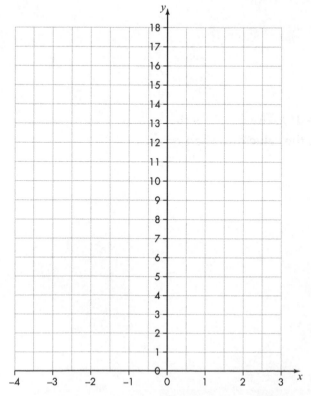

c Use the graph to work out the value of y when $x = 1.5$.

$y =$ _____

2　**a** Complete this table of values for $y = 2x^2 - 4x - 1$.

x	−2	−1	0	1	2	3
y	15	5		−3		

b Draw the graph of $y = 2x^2 - 4x - 1$ on the coordinate grid below.

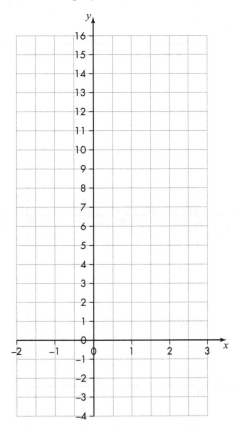

c An approximate solution of the equation $2x^2 - 4x - 1 = 0$ is $x = -0.22$.

　i Explain how you can work this out from your graph.

_____

　ii Use your graph to write down another solution of this equation.

_____

2.13 Recognising shapes of graphs

Look at these graphs.

A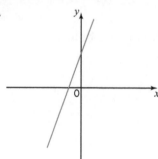

B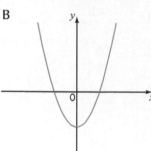

C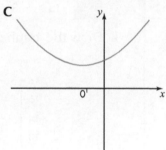

D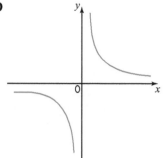

E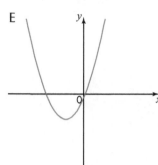

F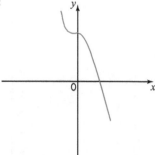

G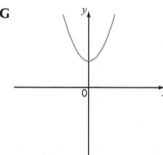

H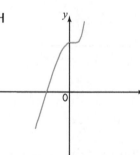

I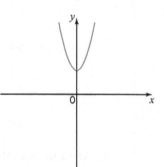

Match each graph to its equation.

1 $y = x^2 + 1$ is graph _____ .

2 $y = 2x^2 + 1$ is graph _____ .

3 $y = x^2 - 1$ is graph _____ .

4 $y = x^2 + 2x$ is graph _____ .

5 $y = 2x + 1$ is graph _____ .

6 $y = x^3 + 1$ is graph _____ .

7 $y = -x^3 + 1$ is graph _____ .

8 $y = \frac{1}{2}x^2 + 2x + 1$ is graph _____ .

9 $y = \frac{1}{x}$ is graph _____ .

2.14 Simultaneous equations

1 Solve each pair of simultaneous equations graphically.

a $y = 2x + 1$
$y = -x + 7$

b $y = -2x + 7$
$2y = x + 4$

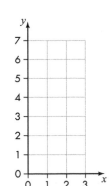

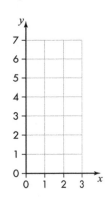

$x =$ _____ $y =$ _____

$x =$ _____ $y =$ _____

2 Solve each pair of simultaneous equations.

a $4x + y = 12$
$5x - y = 6$

b $2y + x = 8$
$y - 2x = -1$

c $5x - 3y = 16$
$2x + 2y = 16$

_____ _____ _____

_____ _____ _____

_____ _____ _____

_____ _____ _____

_____ _____ _____

_____ _____ _____

3 A café sells a total of 300 cakes and muffins in one day.

They make a total of £870 from the cakes and muffins.

Cakes cost £3.50 each and muffins cost £2.50 each.

How many cakes were sold?

_____

_____

_____

_____

_____

3 Ratio, proportion and rates of change

3.1 Sharing an amount in a given ratio

1 Share 50 in the ratio 2 : 3. _____

2 Share 400 g in the ratio 2 : 3. _____

3 Share £90 in the ratio 3 : 7. _____

4 Share 1 km in the ratio 1 : 99. _____

5 Share 100 ml in the ratio 2 : 3 : 5. _____

6 Share 13.5 kg in the ratio 6 : 5 : 1. _____

7 Concrete is made from cement, sand and gravel in the ratio 1 : 2 : 4. Paul needs three and a half tonnes of concrete. How much of each ingredient does he need?

_____

8 Aaron is 6 years old, Beth is 9 years old and Charlie is 15 years old. They are going to share £5940 in the same ratio as their ages.

a How much do they each receive?

_____

b If the money was shared out one year later, how much less would Charlie receive?

_____

9 The sizes of the interior angles of a quadrilateral are in the ratio 2 : 3 : 6 : 7. Calculate the size of the smallest angle.

_____

_____

3.2 Using ratio

1 The ratio of male teachers to female teachers in a primary school is 1 : 9. There are 36 female teachers in the school. How many male teachers are there?

_____

2 The ratio of male teachers to female teachers in a primary school is 8 : 7. There are 32 male teachers in the school. How many teachers are there altogether?

_____

3 The ratio of staff to students in a school is 2 : 35. There are 665 students in the school. How many staff are there?

_____

4 The ratio of staff to Year 10 students to Year 11 students going on a school trip is 2 : 5 : 7. There are 225 Year 10 students on the trip.

a How many Year 11 students are going on the trip?

_____

b How many people are going on the trip altogether?

_____

5 Mahmoud is making a drink from lemonade, orange and ginger in the ratio 40 : 9 : 1. He has 4.5 litres of orange and uses it all. How much of the other ingredients does he use?

_____

6 When the cost of a meal was shared between two families in the ratio 4 : 5, the smaller share was £31. How much did the meal cost altogether?

_____

7 Write the ratio $\cos 60° : \tan 45°$ in the form $1 : n$.

_____

3.3 Direct and indirect proportion

1 T is directly proportional to P.

They are linked by the equation $T = 6P$.

a Calculate the value of T when $P = 3$. _____

b Calculate the value of P when $T = 9$. _____

2 R is inversely proportional to S.

They are linked by the equation $R = \dfrac{2}{S}$.

a Calculate the value of R when $S = 4$. _____

b Calculate the value of S when $R = 6$. _____

3 A is directly proportional to the square of D.

They are linked by the equation $A = 3D^2$.

a Calculate the value of A when $D = 5$. _____

b Calculate the value of D when $A = 108$. _____

4 Here are four graphs.

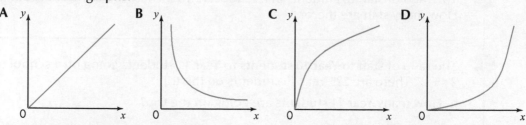

A y B y C y D y

Write down the letter of the graph that could represent the relationship:

a y is proportional to x^2 _____

b y is proportional to x _____

c y is proportional to $\frac{1}{x}$. _____

4 Geometry and measures

4.1 Circles – circumference 📱

1 Calculate the circumference of each circle.

Give all answers correct to one decimal place.

a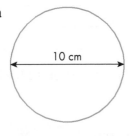

10 cm

_____
_____
_____

b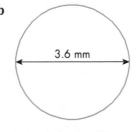

3.6 mm

_____
_____
_____

c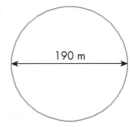

190 m

_____
_____
_____

d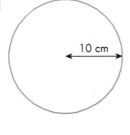

10 cm

_____
_____
_____

e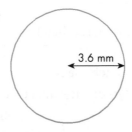

3.6 mm

_____
_____
_____

f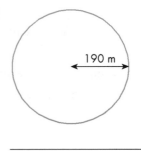

190 m

_____
_____
_____

2 A mountain bicycle wheel has a diameter of 56 cm.

a Work out the circumference of the wheel.

_____
_____

b How many complete revolutions does the wheel make when the bicycle travels 500 m?

_____

c The 'Tour Divide' is the longest mountain bike race in the world. It is approximately 4420 km long. How many complete revolutions does the wheel make when the bicycle completes the 'Tour Divide'?

_____
_____
_____

3 Calculate the circumference of each circle.

Leave all answers in terms of π.

a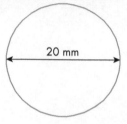
20 mm

b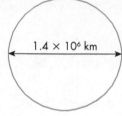
1.4×10^6 km

c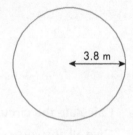
3.8 m

_____

_____

_____

4 A penny-farthing bicycle has a front wheel with a radius of 90 cm and a back wheel with a radius of 20 cm.

In a journey, the front wheel turned 200 times.

How many complete revolutions did the back wheel make?

_____

_____

_____

Hint: Work out the distance travelled first.

5 Calculate the perimeter of each shape.

Give your answers correct to one decimal place.

a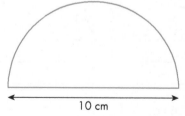
10 cm

b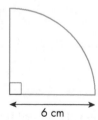
6 cm

_____   _____

_____   _____

_____   _____

Hint: Include the lengths of any straight sides.

6 Calculate the perimeter of each shape.

Give your answers in terms of π.

a

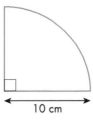

10 cm

b

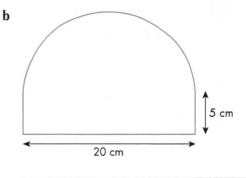

5 cm

20 cm

_____

_____

_____

_____

_____

_____

7 A circle has a circumference of 300 cm.

Calculate the diameter of the circle, correct to one decimal place.

_____

_____

8 A circle has a circumference of 1 m.

Calculate the radius of the circle, correct to two decimal places.

_____

_____

9 Work out the total length of all the lines in this shape. It is made of two circles and three straight lines.

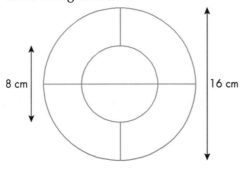

8 cm

16 cm

_____

_____

_____

4.2 Circles – area 🖩

1   Calculate the area of each circle.

Give all answers correct to one decimal place.

a
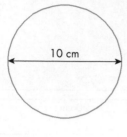
10 cm

_____
_____
_____

b
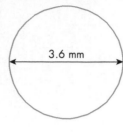
3.6 mm

_____
_____
_____

c
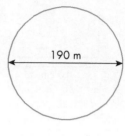
190 m

_____
_____
_____

d
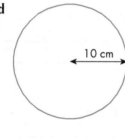
10 cm

_____
_____
_____

e
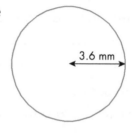
3.6 mm

_____
_____
_____

f
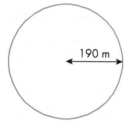
190 m

_____
_____
_____

2   Calculate the area of each circle.

Leave all answers in terms of π.

a
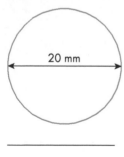
20 mm

_____
_____
_____

b
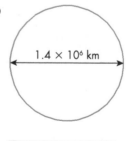
1.4×10^6 km

_____
_____
_____

c
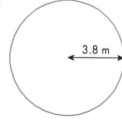
3.8 m

_____
_____
_____

3 Calculate the area of each shape.

Give your answers correct to two decimal places.

a

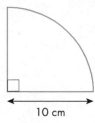

10 cm

b

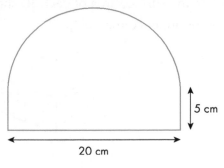

5 cm

20 cm

_____   _____
_____   _____
_____   _____

4 Calculate the area that is shaded in each shape. Give your answers correct to two decimal places.

a

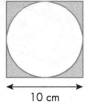

10 cm

b

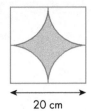

20 cm

c

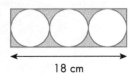

18 cm

_____   _____   _____
_____   _____   _____
_____   _____   _____

5 Work out the area of each shape. They are all made up from semicircles.

Leave all your answers in terms of π.

a

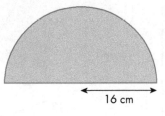

16 cm

b

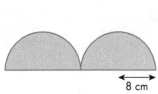

8 cm

c

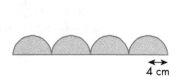

4 cm

_____   _____   _____
_____   _____   _____
_____   _____   _____

d By looking at your answers to parts **a**, **b** and **c**, write down the total area of a shape made up of eight semicircles, each with a radius of 2 cm.

_____

4.3 Prisms and 3D shapes – surface area

Calculate the surface area of each 3D shape.

All lengths are in centimetres.

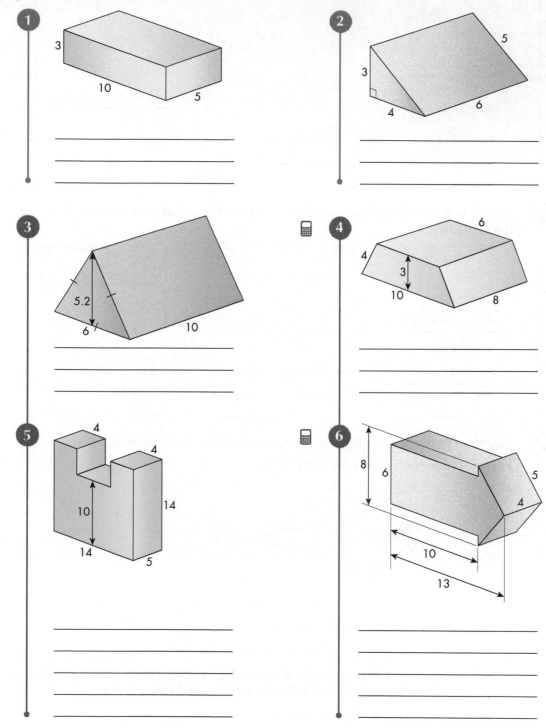

1 3 10 5

2 5 3 4 6

3 5.2 6 10

4 6 4 3 10 8

5 4 4 10 14 14 5

6 8 6 5 4 10 13

Calculate the surface area of each shape.

All lengths are in centimetres. Use the given formulae.

7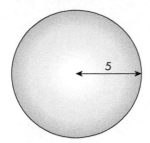

Surface area = $4\pi r^2$

_____

_____

_____

8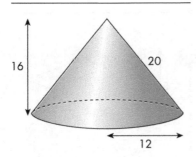

Surface area = $\pi r l + \pi r^2$

_____

_____

_____

9 A4 paper is approximately 21 cm by 30 cm.

What is the maximum number of cylindrical paper tubes of diameter 3 cm and height 6 cm that can be made from a piece of A4 paper?

_____

_____

_____

_____

4.4 Prisms and 3D shapes – volume 🖩

Calculate the volume of each 3D shape.

All lengths are in centimetres.

1

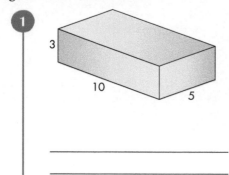

_____

_____

_____

2

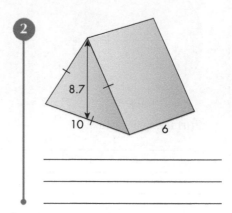

_____

_____

_____

3

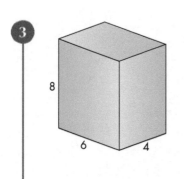

_____

_____

_____

4

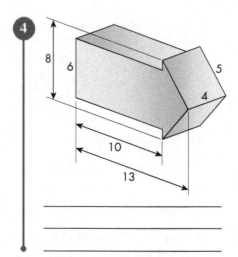

_____

_____

_____

5

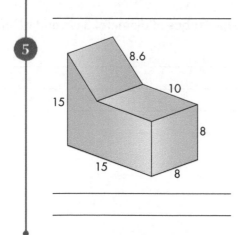

_____

_____

_____

6

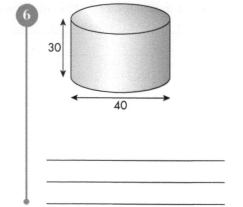

_____

_____

_____

7 A plastic hosepipe is 25 m long.

Its external diameter is 15 mm. Its internal diameter is 12 mm.

Calculate the volume of plastic that makes the hosepipe.

Remember: Think of your units.

_____

_____

_____

_____

8 The diagram shows a cuboid A and a right-angled triangular prism B.

A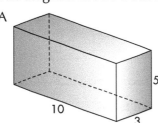

B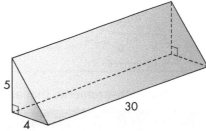

Show that the volume of B is twice the volume of A.

_____

_____

_____

_____

Calculate the volume of each shape.

All lengths are in centimetres. Use the given formulae.

9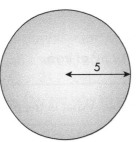

Volume $= \frac{4}{3}\pi r^3$

_____

_____

_____

10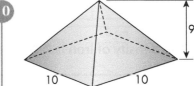

Volume $= \frac{1}{3}$ base area $\times h$

_____

_____

_____

5 Triangle ABE is similar to ACD.

Calculate the lengths x and y.

a $x =$ _____

b $y =$ _____

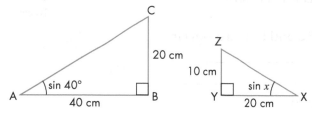

6 A mobile phone mast is 18 m high. At 11:00 am it casts a shadow 32 m long. At the same time, an electricity pylon near to the mast casts a shadow 56 m long. Calculate the height of the pylon.

> Hint: A quick sketch will probably help.

_____

_____

_____

7 Triangle ABC is similar to XYZ.

C
20 cm
Z
10 cm
sin 40°
A   40 cm   B
sin x
Y   20 cm   X

Write down the value of x. _____

4.7 Congruent triangles

Remember:

There are four types of congruency:

SSS, SAS, ASA and RHS.

 1 State whether the triangles in each pair are congruent. Give reasons for your answer.

a
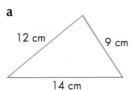 

_____
_____
_____

b
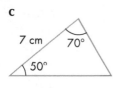 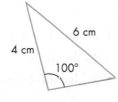

_____
_____
_____

c
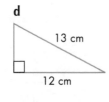 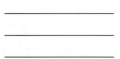

_____
_____
_____

d
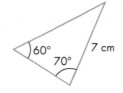 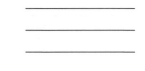

_____
_____
_____

 2 ABCD is a kite.

Draw in the diagonals AC and BD. Label the intersection E.

Which triangles are congruent to each other? Give your reasons. _____

_____
_____
_____
_____

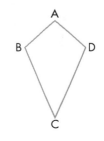

3 PQRS is a rhombus.

Draw in the diagonals PR and QS. Label the intersection T.

Which triangles are congruent to each other? Give your reasons.

_____
_____
_____

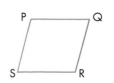

4.8 Trigonometry

1 Use the appropriate trigonometric ratio to calculate the values marked x in the triangles.

a

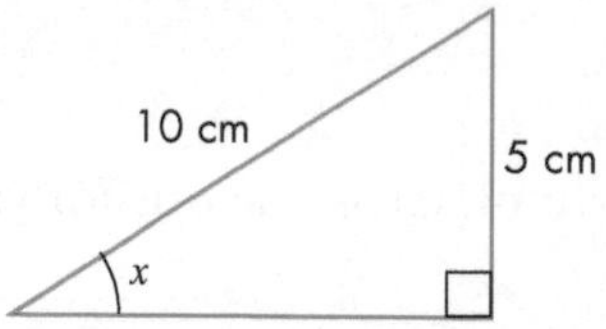

10 cm 5 cm x

b

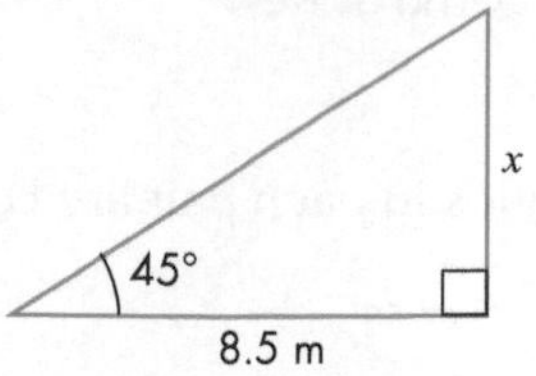

x 45° 8.5 m

c

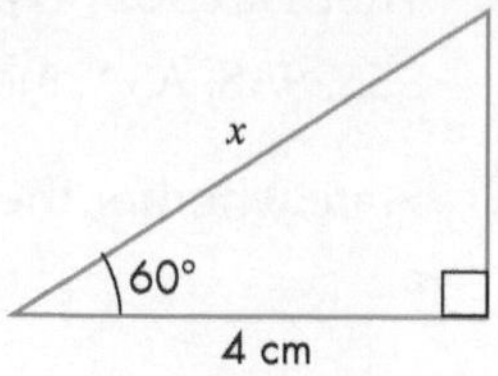

x 60° 4 cm

_____

_____

_____

2 A ladder, 4.75 m long, rests against a wall.

The foot of the ladder is 2 m from the base of the wall.

What angle does the ladder make with the floor?

Give your answer correct to three significant figures.

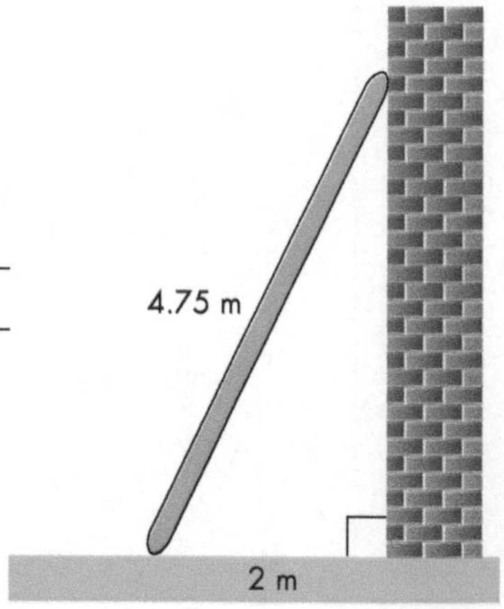

_____

_____

4.75 m

2 m

3 A ship leaves port A and sails on a bearing of 25° for 50 km.

How far east of port A is the ship?

Hint: A quick sketch will probably help.

_____

_____

4 Calculate the area of the isosceles triangle. Start by working out the perpendicular height.

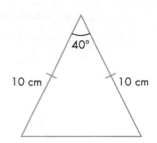

_____

_____

_____

_____

_____

4.9 Arcs and sectors

1 Calculate the arc length of each sector, correct to three significant figures.

a

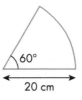

60°

20 cm

b

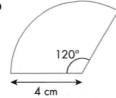

120°

4 cm

c

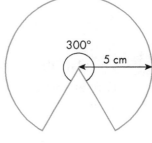

300°

5 cm

_____   _____   _____

_____   _____   _____

_____   _____   _____

2 Calculate the area of each sector, giving your answers in terms of π.

a

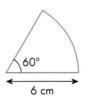

60°

6 cm

b

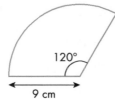

120°

9 cm

c

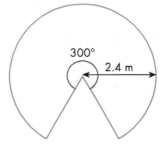

300°

2.4 m

_____   _____   _____

_____   _____   _____

_____   _____   _____

3　**a** Work out the area of the shaded region of the shape.

　　Give your answer correct to two decimal places.

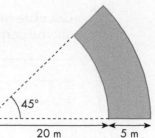

_____

_____

_____

　b Work out the perimeter of the shaded region of the shape.

　　Give the answer in terms of π.

_____

_____

_____

4.10 Pythagoras' theorem　

1　Calculate the length, x, in each triangle.

　Give answers correct to one decimal place where necessary.

a

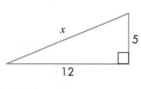

b

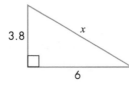

c

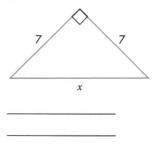

_____　　_____　　_____

_____　　_____　　_____

_____　　_____　　_____

2　Calculate the length, x, in each triangle.

　Give answers correct to one decimal place where necessary.

a

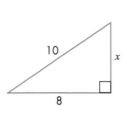

b

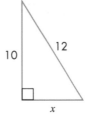

c

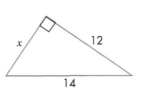

_____　　_____　　_____

_____　　_____　　_____

_____　　_____　　_____

3　Calculate the length of the diagonal of a square of side 10 cm.

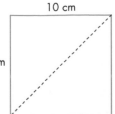

_____

_____

_____

4 Calculate the length of the diagonal of Stamford Bridge's football pitch.

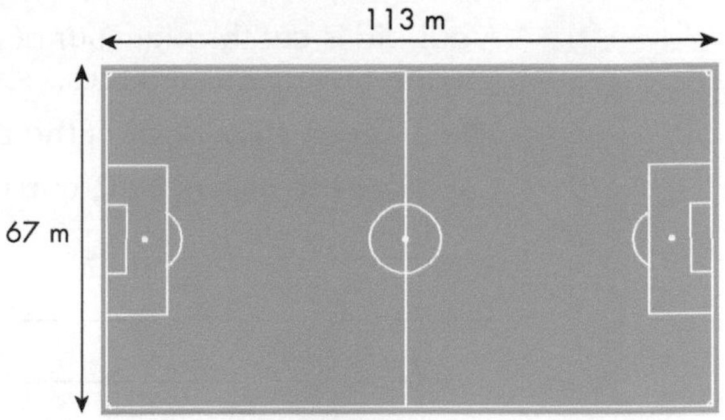

_____

_____

_____

113 m

67 m

5 A ladder, 6 m long, leans against a wall.

The ladder reaches 5 m up the wall.

How far from the base of the wall is the foot of the ladder?

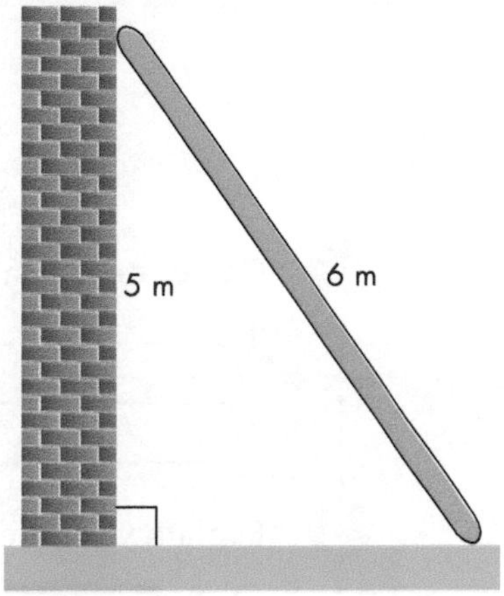

_____

_____

_____

5 m   6 m

6 A right-angled triangle with shorter sides of 5 cm and 9 cm is inside a circle with centre O.

Calculate the radius of the circle.

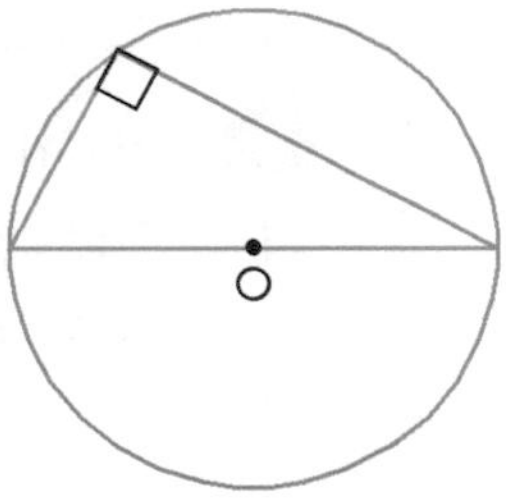

_____

_____

_____

O

7 Calculate the length of the line segment AB, correct to the nearest whole number when:

a A is at point (3, 4) and B is at (5, 9)

_____

_____

_____

b A is at point (−3, 1) and B is at (4, −2).

_____

_____

_____

8 A cuboid is cut through four of its vertices A, B, C and D leaving two identical pieces.

The diagram shows one of the pieces.

Calculate the distance AC, correct to two decimal places.

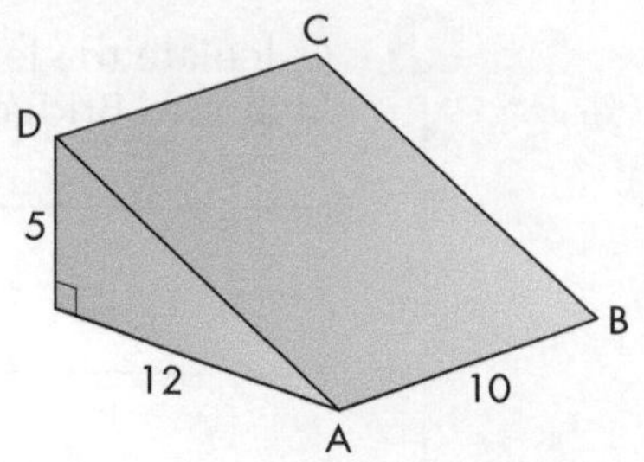

_____

_____

_____

_____

4.11 Regular polygons 🖩

1 Calculate: **a** the interior angle   **b** the exterior angle of a regular pentagon.

a _____   **b** _____

_____   _____

_____   _____

2 Explain why the sum of the internal angles of a hexagon is 720°.

_____

_____

3 The diagram shows part of a regular polygon.

The external angle is 45°.

How many sides does the polygon have altogether?

45°

_____

_____

4 The interior angles of a regular polygon are 160°.

Explain why the polygon must have 18 sides.

_____

_____

5 Work out the values of a, b and c in this regular hexagon.

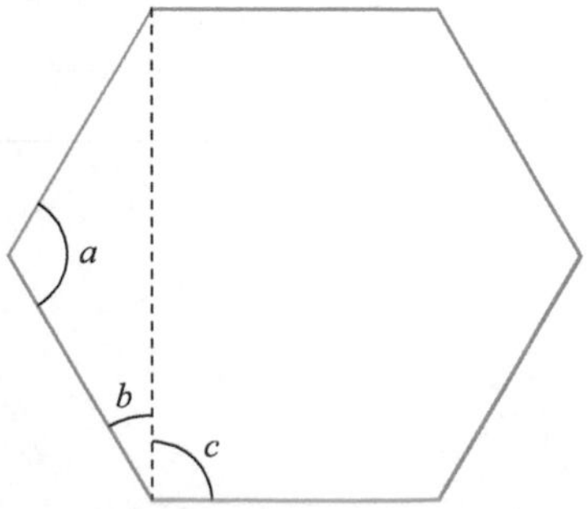

_____

_____

_____

a

b

c

6 A carpenter is making a seat to fit around a post. The seat is in the shape of a regular nonagon (nine-sided shape).

The diagram shows a plan view of the seat. What angle must the carpenter cut the wood, marked *a* on the diagram, for the seat?

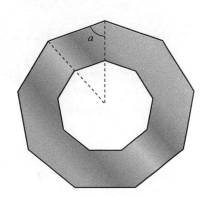

_____

_____

4.12 Translation

1

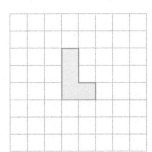

a Translate the shape three squares right and one square down.

b Translate the shape one square left and two squares up.

2 **a** Describe the translation that maps A onto C.

_____

b Describe the translation that maps B onto C.

_____

c Describe the translation that maps B onto A.

_____

d Describe the translation that maps C onto A.

_____

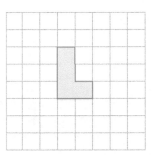

3 Write down the column vector for each translation.

a Shape D to shape A _____

b Shape E to shape D _____

c Shape C to shape B _____

d Shape A to shape D _____

e Shape B to shape A _____

f Shape A to shape C _____

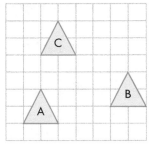

4.13 More vectors

1 On a grid, $\begin{pmatrix} 3 \\ -1 \end{pmatrix}$ translates shape P onto shape Q and $\begin{pmatrix} 3 \\ 3 \end{pmatrix}$ translates shape Q onto shape R.

Write down the column vector that translates shape P directly onto shape R.

_____

2 $p = \begin{pmatrix} 4 \\ 2 \end{pmatrix}$ $q = \begin{pmatrix} -1 \\ 3 \end{pmatrix}$ $r = \begin{pmatrix} -1 \\ -2 \end{pmatrix}$

a On the squared grid below, draw diagrams to illustrate these vectors.

  i **p**   **ii** **q**   **iii** **r**

  iv **p + q**   **v** **2r**   **vi** **2r + p**

b Write these vectors as column vectors.

  i **p + r** = _____   **ii** **q + r** = _____

  iii **p − q** = _____   **iv** **q − r** = _____

  v **2p** = _____   **vi** **3q** = _____

  vii **−r** = _____   **viii** **3q − r** = _____

4.14 Rotation

1

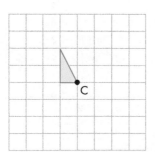

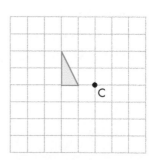

a Draw the image of the shape after a rotation of $\frac{1}{4}$ turn clockwise about centre C.

b Draw the image of the shape after a rotation of 180° about centre C.

2   **a** Draw the image of the shape after a rotation 90° clockwise about the point (0, 0).

b Draw the image of the shape after a rotation 90° anticlockwise about the point (1, −3).

c Draw the image of the shape after a rotation 180° about the point (−1, −1).

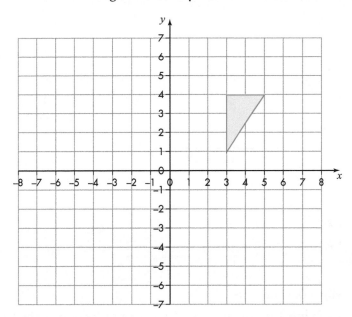

3   Rotate the shapes about centre (0, 0) to make a pattern with rotational symmetry of order four.

a

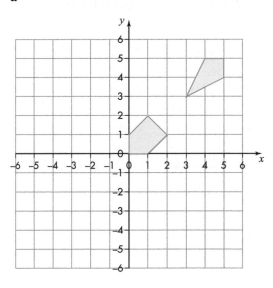

b

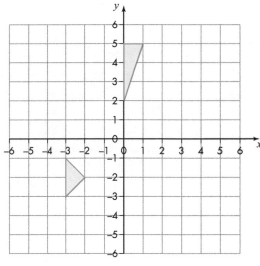

4.15 Reflection

1 Draw the reflection of each shape in the line $y = 1$.

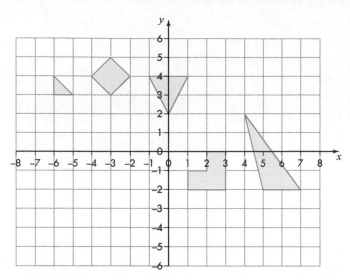

2 a Draw the line $y = x$ with a dashed line.

  b Draw the reflection of shape A in the line $y = x$. Label the reflection shape W.

  c Draw the reflection of shape B in the line $y = x$. Label the reflection shape X.

  d Draw the reflection of shape C in the line $y = x$. Label the reflection shape Y.

  e Draw the reflection of shape D in the line $y = x$. Label the reflection shape Z.

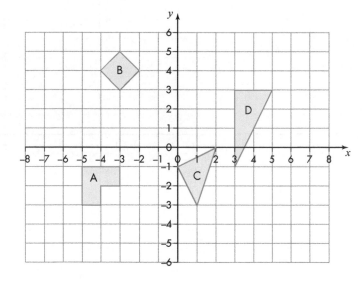

3 Describe the transformation that takes:

a shape A to shape B _____

_____

b shape E to shape F _____

_____

c shape P to shape Q _____

_____

d shape X to shape Y _____

_____

e shape Y to shape X. _____

_____

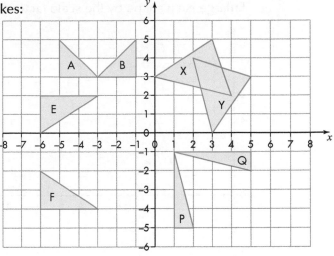

4.16 Enlargement

1 Enlarge the shape by a scale factor of three with (0, 0) as the centre of enlargement.

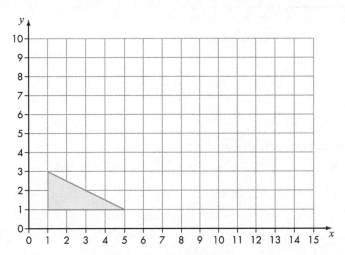

2 Enlarge each shape by a scale factor of 2, using C as the centre of enlargement.

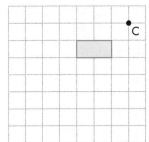
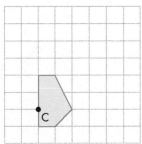

3 Enlarge each shape by the scale factor given, using C as the centre of enlargement.

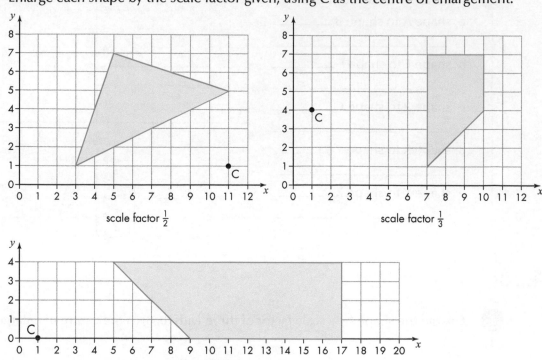

scale factor $\frac{1}{2}$

scale factor $\frac{1}{3}$

scale factor $\frac{1}{4}$

4.17 Constructions

1 Make an accurate drawing of each shape.

a

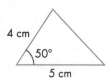

4 cm
50°
5 cm

b

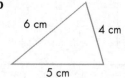

6 cm
4 cm
5 cm

c

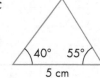

40° 55°
5 cm

d

5 cm
110°
5 cm
70°
5 cm

2 Using a pair of compasses and a ruler, construct an angle of 60° at point A.

A •————————————

3 Using a pair of compasses and a straight edge, construct the perpendicular bisector of the line segment AB.

A————————————— B

4 Using a pair of compasses and a ruler, construct the angle bisector of ABC.

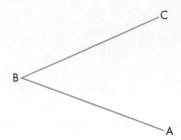

5 Using a pair of compasses and a straight edge, construct the perpendicular bisector of the line that passes through point A.

6   Using a pair of compasses and a ruler, construct a right angle that passes through point A from the line.

A.

_____

4.18 Loci

1   Draw the locus of points that are 2 cm from point X.

X.

2 Draw the locus of points that are 2 cm from XY.

X  Y

3 Draw the locus of points that are 2 cm from this line.

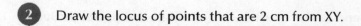

4 Geometry and measures

4 A goat is tethered to the corner of a shed by a rope that is 4 m long. Show on the diagram all of the ground that the goat could reach. Use a scale of 1 cm = 1 m.

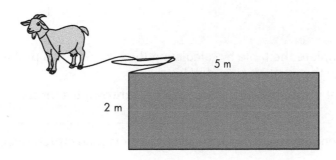

5 m

2 m

5 **a** Construct the locus of points inside the trapezium that are equidistant from AD and CD.

b Construct the locus of points inside the trapezium that are 2 cm from AD.

c Construct the locus of points inside the trapezium that are 5 cm from A.

d Shade the region inside the trapezium where points are nearer to CD than to AD, within 2 cm of AD and more than 5 cm from A.

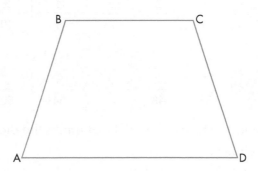

5 Probability

5.1 Basic probability

1 Nemah throws a dice and records the number of threes that he gets after various numbers of throws.

Number of throws	10	50	100	200	500	1000
Number of threes	3	6	19	30	92	163
Experimental probability						

a Complete the table by calculating the experimental probability of a three at each stage that Nemah recorded his results.

b What is the theoretical probability of throwing a three?

_____

c If Nemah threw the dice 6000 times, how many threes would you expect him to get?

_____

2 A coin is flipped 1000 times. How many times would you expect the coin to land 'heads'?

_____

3 I have a bag containing 30 balls, 15 of which are blue, 10 are red and five are green. I take out a ball at random, note its colour and put it back in the bag. I do this 300 times. How many times would I expect to get:

a a red ball _____

b a blue or a green ball _____

c a ball that is not green _____

d a yellow ball? _____

4 Crawford and Janet each carry out an experiment with the same dice. The tables show their results.

Crawford's results

Number	1	2	3	4	5	6
Frequency	6	4	13	9	10	8

Janet's results

Number	1	2	3	4	5	6
Frequency	53	48	45	54	50	52

Crawford thinks the dice is biased. Janet thinks the dice is fair. Who is correct? Explain your choice.

_____

_____

5 A card is taken at random from a shuffled pack of ordinary cards.

   a What is the probability it is red? _____

   b What is the probability it is black? _____

   c Explain why the outcomes in part **a** and **b** are mutually exclusive.

   _____

   _____

   d Explain why the outcomes in part **a** and **b** are exhaustive.

   _____

   _____

6 **a** List the possible outcomes when three coins are thrown together. One has been done for you.

   HHH, _____

   b What is the probability of throwing three heads? _____

   c What is the probability of throwing two heads and one tail? _____

7 **a** List the possible outcomes when one coin and one ordinary dice are thrown together. One has been done for you.

   H1, _____

   b What is the probability of throwing one tail and a 4? _____

8 A fair six-sided dice is thrown twice.

   What is the probability of throwing a one and then a two? _____

9 Two four-sided dice are thrown together and their scores are added.

   a Draw a sample space diagram showing the possible outcomes.

   b What is the probability of throwing a total of six? _____

10 When a coin is thrown and a four-sided dice is thrown at the same time, what is the probability of throwing a tail on the coin and a two on the dice?

   _____

   _____

11 The probabilities of whether students at a school, picked at random, are vegetarian or not are shown in the table.

	Boys	Girls
Vegetarian	0.07	0.2
Not vegetarian	0.42	0.31

a What is the probability that a student chosen at random is a vegetarian?

_____

b In the whole school, there are 170 girls who are vegetarian. How many students are there in the school altogether?

_____

c How many non-vegetarian boys are there in the school altogether?

_____

12 a A 10p coin and a 50p coin are thrown at the same time.

Draw a probability tree diagram to show all the possible outcomes.

> Hint: Remember to write the probabilities along each branch.

10p   **50p**

b Use your probability tree diagram to work out:

i P(two heads) _____

ii P(one head then one tail) _____

iii P(one head and one tail) _____

iv P(at least one head). _____

13 A bag contains four toffees and six chocolates. All the sweets look identical.

Adrian takes and eats a sweet at random. He then takes and eats another sweet at random.

a Draw a probability tree diagram to show all the possible outcomes.

First sweet   **Second sweet**

Use your probability tree diagram to work out the probability that:

b Adrian picks two toffees _____

c Adrian picks at least one toffee _____

d Adrian does not pick a toffee. _____

5.2 Frequency trees

50 students practised taking penalties.

30 were predicted to score a goal.

24 of those predicted to score actually scored.

32 students scored altogether.

Complete the frequency tree.

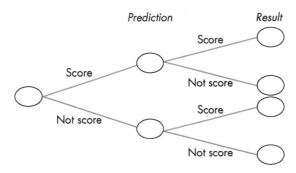

2 400 students took a test.

320 were predicted to pass.

10 of those predicted not to pass actually passed.

310 students passed altogether.

a Complete the frequency tree.

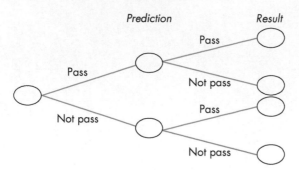

b What percentage of students did not pass? _____

5.3 Venn diagrams

1 Look at the Venn diagram.

50 students were asked about their pets.

36 owned a dog, 16 owned a cat and 30 students owned a dog but not a cat.

Complete the Venn diagram.

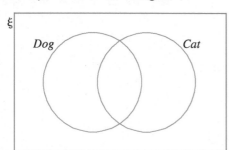

2 35 scuba divers were asked where they had dived.

22 of the 35 had dived in the Irish Sea (I).

15 of the 35 had dived in the Red Sea (R).

9 of the 35 had dived in both the Irish Sea and the Red Sea.

a Draw a Venn diagram to show this information.

b Work out the probability that a randomly selected diver has not dived in either the Irish Sea or the Red Sea.

_____

c Work out P($I \cup R$). _____

3 The Venn diagram shows the number of people in a park walking dogs (D) and the number wearing coats (C).

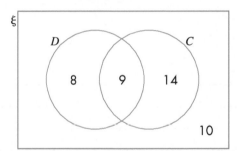

a How many people are in the park? _____

b What is the probability that someone chosen at random is wearing a coat?

_____

c Work out P(C'). _____

d Work out P($D \cap C$). _____

e Work out P($D \cup C$). _____

f Work out the probability that someone in the park has a dog but not a coat.

_____

6 Statistics

6.1 Mean, median, mode and range 🖩

1 These are the salaries for all eight people working in a small company.

£8000, £18 000, £18 000, £18 000, £24 000, £24 000, £25 000, £37 000

a Calculate the range. _____

b Write down the modal salary. _____

c Work out the median salary. _____

d Calculate the mean salary. _____

_____

Everyone in the company gets a £2000 pay rise. What is the new:

e range of salaries _____   f modal salary _____

g median salary _____   h mean salary? _____

2 Look at the frequency table.

x	Frequency
2	7
3	3
4	5
5	6

a Calculate the range. _____

b Write down the mode. _____

c Work out the median. _____

d Calculate the mean. _____

_____

3 Look at the frequency table.

Shoe size	3	4	5	6	7	8	9
Number of students	4	9	12	19	10	4	2

a Calculate the range. _____

b Write down the mode. _____

c Work out the median. _____

d Calculate the mean. _____

_____

4 Students at a school are awarded merits for good work. This table shows the numbers of merits awarded to the students in three different year groups in one month.

Number of merits	Year 7 frequency	Year 8 frequency	Year 9 frequency
0	14	4	24
1	17	22	38
2	42	30	20
3	24	33	13
4	8	17	11
5	4	16	7
6	15	8	10

a How many students are there in Year 7? _____

b Calculate the mean number of merits awarded per student for the students in Year 7. Give your answer correct to two decimal places.

_____

_____

5 Look at the grouped frequency table.

x	$0 < x \leqslant 5$	$5 < x \leqslant 10$	$10 < x \leqslant 15$	$15 < x \leqslant 20$
Frequency	16	27	19	13

a Write down the modal class. _____

b Calculate an estimate of the mean. _____

_____

6 Look at the grouped frequency table.

x	Frequency
$0 < x \leqslant 10$	4
$10 < x \leqslant 20$	9
$20 < x \leqslant 30$	17
$30 < x \leqslant 40$	13
$40 < x \leqslant 50$	7

a Write down the modal class. _____

b Calculate an estimate of the mean. _____

_____

c Why can't you work out the range for this data?

_____

_____

7 A list of nine numbers has a mean of 4.8.

What number must be added to give a new mean of five?

_____

_____

8 The mean mass of five basketball players is 68.4 kg. The mean mass of the five basketball players and their coach is 71 kg.

What is the mass of the coach?

_____

_____

9 The mean mass of a junior team of 15 rugby players is 78.5 kg. A player who weighs 71.2 kg leaves the team and is replaced by a player who weighs 75.7 kg.

What is the new mean mass of the team?

_____

_____

10 The numbers of homeworks given to some students are listed in a frequency table. The frequency in the last row has been covered by a tea stain!

Homeworks given	Frequency
0	6
1	3
2	8
3	7
4	●

The median number of homeworks is 2.5.

Calculate the mean number of homeworks given.

Give your answer correct to two decimal places.

_____

_____

_____

_____

_____

6.2 Bar charts

1 The table shows how the 30 students in Class 11a travel to school.

Bus	Car	Taxi	Walk
11	7	2	10

Draw a bar chart to show this information.

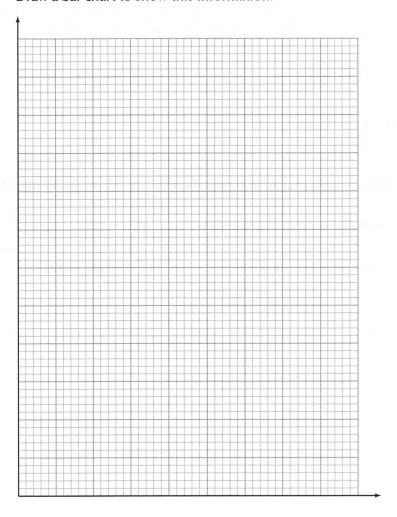

2 The table shows the numbers of cars sold at a garage in one week.

Day of week	Monday	Tuesday	Wednesday	Thursday	Friday
Number of cars sold	9	10	11	10	12

Sam uses this information to draw a this bar chart.

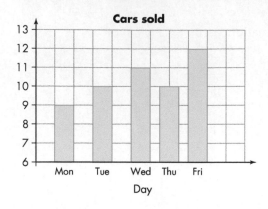

a A customer looks at the bar chart and says: 'Twice as many cars were sold on Friday as on Monday.'

Is the customer correct? Show how you decide.

_____

b Another customer says: 'This bar chart has not been drawn properly.'

Write down **two** mistakes that Sam has made.

Mistake 1

_____

Mistake 2

_____

6.3 Pie charts

1 The pie chart shows the numbers of dogs owned by people who took part in a survey.

Number of dogs owned

(pie chart with sections labelled: 1 dog, 2 dogs, No dogs, More than 2 dogs)

a What percentage of those surveyed owned 2 dogs? _____

b Make a comparison between the number of people who did not own a dog and those that did.

_____

_____

c What fraction of those surveyed owned more than 2 dogs? _____

d 200 people in the survey said they owned 1 dog. How many people in total were surveyed?

_____

_____

6.4 Correlation

Miss Directed is investigating this claim about Ford motor cars.

'The older the car, the less it is worth.'

Miss Directed collects some data from a local newspaper and draws a scatter diagram to show her results.

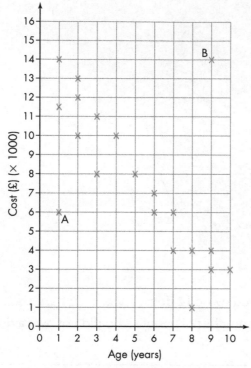

Miss Directed sees three more cars to add to her data:

three years old, valued at £10 000

three years old, valued at £9000

seven years old, valued at £5500

a Plot these points onto the scatter diagram.

b Decide whether the claim 'the older the car, the less it is worth', is correct.

_____

c Cars A and B do not fit the general trend. What can you say about:

  i car A _____

  ii car B? _____

d Do you think that this general trend continues as cars get even older? Explain your answer.

_____

2 Mr Stephens is investigating this claim.

> 'The greater the percentage attendance at my maths lessons, the higher the mark in the end of year maths test.'

Mr Stephens collects data from his class and draws a scatter diagram to show his results.

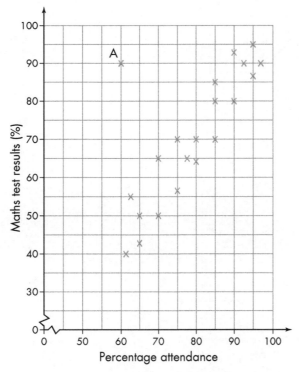

a Decide whether the claim 'the greater the percentage attendance at my maths lessons, the higher the mark in the end of year maths test', is correct or not.

_____

b Student A does not fit the general trend. What can you say about student A?

_____

c Describe the correlation between percentage attendance and the maths test result.

_____

d Draw a line of best fit on the scatter diagram.

e Use your line of best fit to estimate:

   i the maths result of a student with an 85% attendance _____

   ii the attendance of a student with a test result of 60%. _____

f Why would it not be useful to use the line of best fit to estimate the test mark for a student with a 40% attendance?

_____

3 The table shows the scores of some students in a mental test and a written test.

Student	Amy	Billy	Chris	Dom	Eddy	Flynn	Glyn	Harjit	Iris	Jill
Mental	13	17	22	25	20	14	14	18	12	21
Written	25	30	34	13	37	29	25	44	19	35

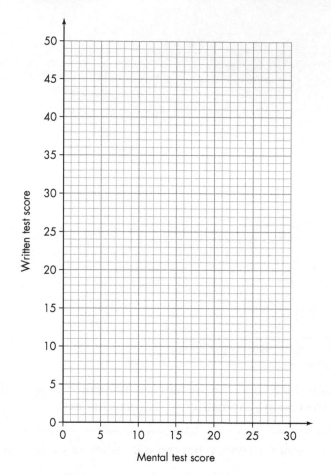

a Plot the data on a scatter graph on the axes provided.

b Draw a line of best fit.

c Keith missed the mental test, but scored 32 on the written test. Estimate the score that Keith would have got on the mental test.

_____

d One person did not do as well as expected on the written test. Who do you think that was? Give a reason for your choice.

_____

e Describe the correlation between the two types of test.

_____

6.5 Time series graphs

1   Neil recorded his mass at the end of each two-week period, for the first 10 weeks of his diet.

Week	Start	2	4	6	8	10
Mass (kg)	84.7	83.7	82.5	81.7	81.0	80.3

  a   Draw a line graph for the data.

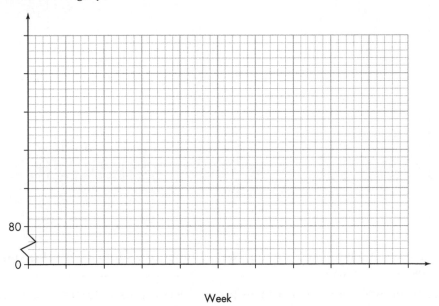

Week

  b   Use your graph to estimate Neil's mass at the end of week 3. _____ kg

  c   In which two-week period did Neil lose the most mass? _____

  d   Comment on the trend of the data. _____

  e   Can you predict Neil's mass at the end of week 14? Give a reason for your answer.

    _____

    _____

2   The table shows the numbers of overseas visitors to London from 2008 to 2013.

Year	2008	2009	2010	2011	2012	2013
Number of visitors (millions)	14.8	14.2	14.7	15.3	15.5	16.8

a Draw a line graph for the data.

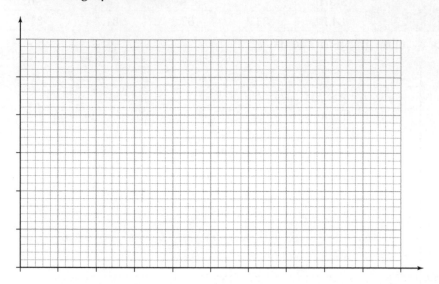

b Use your graph to estimate the likely number of visitors in 2014. Explain how you chose your answer. _____

c Between which two years did visitor numbers increase the most? _____

d Explain the trend in the number of visitors to London. What reasons can you give to explain this trend?

_____

e Is it possible to use this data to predict the likely number of visitors in 2020?

_____

Formulae sheet

Perimeter, area, surface area and volume formulae

Where r is the radius of the sphere or cone, l is the slant height of a cone and h is the perpendicular height of a cone:

$$\text{Curved surface area of a cone} = \pi r l$$

$$\text{Surface area of a sphere} = 4\pi r^2$$

$$\text{Volume of a sphere} = \frac{4}{3}\pi r^3$$

$$\text{Volume of a cone} = \frac{1}{3}\pi r^2 h$$

Kinematics formulae

Where a is constant acceleration, u is initial velocity, v is final velocity, s is displacement from the position when $t = 0$ and t is time:

$$v = u + at$$

$$s = ut + \frac{1}{2}at^2$$

$$v^2 = u^2 + 2as$$

Revision paper 1

1 Use approximations to estimate the value of each expression.

a $\dfrac{1.8 \times 51.3}{7.3 - 2.21}$

_____
_____
_____ **(3)**

b $\dfrac{415.1 + 47.49}{5.383 \times 1.922}$

_____
_____ **(3)**

2 A catering company always provides at least one vegetarian pizza for every eight guests attending a party.

Work out the minimum number of vegetarian pizzas they will supply for 90 guests.

_____
_____

(3)

3 Here is a pattern of lines.

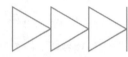

Pattern 1   Pattern 2   Pattern 3

Work out how many lines there will be in the *n*th pattern.

_____

(2)

4 The *n*th term of a sequence is $2n + 8$.

a Show that all the terms in the sequence are even.

_____
_____

(2)

b Which term of the sequence is 26?

_____

(2)

c Write down the *n*th term of this fractional sequence.

$\dfrac{1}{35}, \dfrac{5}{32}, \dfrac{9}{29}, \dfrac{13}{26}, \dfrac{17}{23}, \cdots$

_____
_____

(4)

5 Solve the inequality $4a - 3 < 17$.

_____
_____

(2)

6 Write 540 as a product of its prime factors in index form.

_____

_____

_____

_____

_____

_____

(3)

7 In 2008 a florist sold 1000 orchids for £10 each.

In 2009 the florist sold 20% more orchids than he did in 2008, but the price he got for each orchid was 20% less than in 2008.

Did the florist take the same amount of money in 2009 as in 2008?

You must show your working.

_____

_____

_____

_____

_____

_____

(4)

8 Triangle A is drawn on the grid.

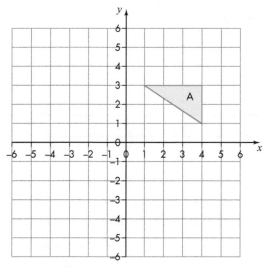

a Draw the image of triangle A after a rotation of 90° anticlockwise about the point (0, 1).

Label the image B.

(3)

b Triangle A is reflected to form a new triangle C. The vertices of triangle C are at (4, –3), (4, –5) and (1, –5). Work out the equation of the mirror line.

_____

_____

(2)

c Enlarge triangle A by scale factor $\frac{1}{2}$, using (–4, –3) as the centre of enlargement. Label the image D.

(2)

d Draw the image of triangle A after a translation by the vector $\begin{pmatrix} -4 \\ -6 \end{pmatrix}$. Label the image E.

(2)

9 Josie says: 'All the terms in the sequence with nth term $n^2 + 2$ are even.'

Give a counter-example to show that she is wrong.

_____

(1)

10 A botanist measures the heights of some young plants.

He writes that the heights of the plants, h, lie in the interval:

$30 \text{ cm} \leqslant h < 35 \text{ cm}$

a Write down all the possible whole-number heights of the plants.

_____

(1)

b Show the inequality $30 \leqslant w < 35$ on this number line.

```
 ┬  ┬  ┬  ┬  ┬  ┬  ┬  ┬  ┬  ┬  ┬
27 28 29 30 31 32 33 34 35 36 37
```

(1)

11 **a** Work out $\sqrt[3]{12^2 - 19}$.

_____

_____

(1)

b Carys writes $6^{15} \div 6^5 = 6^3$.

Is Carys correct? Give a reason for your answer.

_____

_____

(1)

12 **a** Complete the table of values for $y = x^2 - 2x + 2$ for values of x from -3 to 3.

x	-3	-2	-1	0	1	2	3
y	17		5	2		2	

(2)

b Draw the graph of $y = x^2 - 2x + 2$ for values of x from -3 to 3.

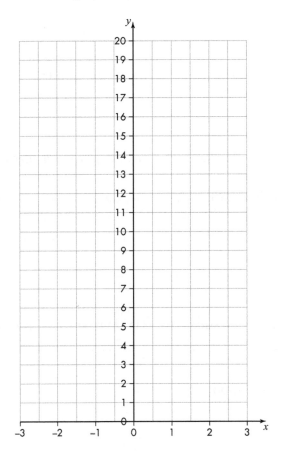

(3)

c Use your graph to estimate the value of y when $x = 2.5$.

_____

(1)

d Use your graph to solve the equation $x^2 - 2x + 2 = 4$.

_____

(2)

13 **a** A ship leaves port P and sails on a bearing of 220° for 6 km to a point A.

At point A the ship changes direction and sails 8 km on a bearing of 075° to point B.

i Using a scale of 1 cm = 1 km, draw a diagram to show the ship's journey.

P.

(2)

ii Measure and write down the distance the ship must travel, and the bearing, to return directly from point B to port.

_____

(2)

b Using only a pair of compasses and a ruler, construct the perpendicular from the point B to the line.

You must show your construction lines.

B.

_____

(2)

14 a Jack says: '$\sqrt{9}$ is a surd as it contains a square root.' Explain why Jack is wrong.

_____

(1)

Give the exact answer to each calculation.

b $\sqrt{2} \times \sqrt{6}$ _____ (1)

c $\sqrt{6} \div \sqrt{2}$ _____ (2)

15 You can model an adult's head as a sphere with a radius of 9.24 cm.

a Work out an estimate for the surface area of an adult's head. Give your answer in square centimetres (cm²).

_____

_____

(2)

b Without carrying out a further calculation, give evidence to show whether your method gives you an underestimate or an overestimate for the surface area of an adult's head.

_____

(2)

TOTAL MARKS _____ / (64)

Revision paper 2 ⊞   Name _____ Date _____

1 The cost of a new lorry is £22 000 + 20% VAT. Pat decides to buy on credit. She pays an initial deposit of 15% and then makes 24 monthly payments of £1000.

How much more does Pat pay by buying on credit? You must show your working.

_____

_____

_____

_____

(4)

2 An estate agent collects information about the average prices of one-bedroom flats at certain distances from the local railway station. The table shows her results.

Distance from railway station (miles)	1	7	3	9	16	12
Average price (£000s)	162	139	156	130	118	124

a On the graph provided, draw a scatter diagram to show this information.

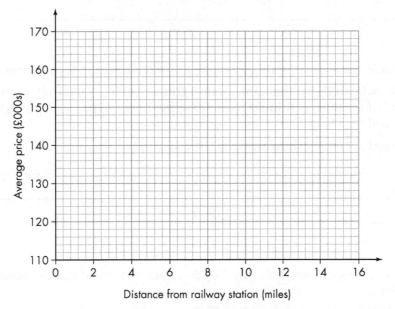

Distance from railway station (miles)

(2)

b Write down the type of correlation shown by your scatter diagram.

_____

(1)

c Draw a line of best fit on your scatter diagram.   **(1)**

d Jordan needs to catch the train to go to work. She has £150 000 to spend on a one-bedroom flat. Use your line of best fit to estimate how close to the railway station she could buy a flat.

_____

(1)

e Why would it not be useful to use the line of best fit to estimate the cost of a one-bedroom flat 24 miles from the railway station?

_____

(1)

3 a Solve the equation $7x + 12 = 39 - 3x$.

_____
_____
_____

(3)

b Expand $x(3x - 4)$.

_____

(2)

c Expand and simplify $4(3d + 2) - 3(d - 2)$.

_____
_____

(3)

d Expand and simplify $(x + 2)(x - 6)$.

_____

(2)

4 In 2009, a biologist estimated that a termite mound contained 520 000 termites.

In 2010 she estimated that the same mound contained 546 000 termites. She said: 'If the number of termites continues to increase by the same percentage each year, by 2015 there will be about 700 000 termites in the mound.'

Do you agree? You must show working to support your answer.

_____
_____
_____

(3)

5 a The table shows the amounts spent by 50 customers at a shop one Saturday in October.

Amount spent, x (£)	Frequency
$0 \leqslant x < 10$	23
$10 \leqslant x < 20$	14
$20 \leqslant x < 30$	9
$30 \leqslant x < 40$	4

a Work out the probability that a customer chosen at random spent less than £20.

_____

(2)

b Explain why it is not possible to work out the probability that a customer chosen at random spent exactly £15.

_____

(1)

c Altogether the shop had 2000 customers in October. How many of them would you expect to have spent between £20 and £30?

_____

(2)

6 Circle the vector that translates shape E to shape F.

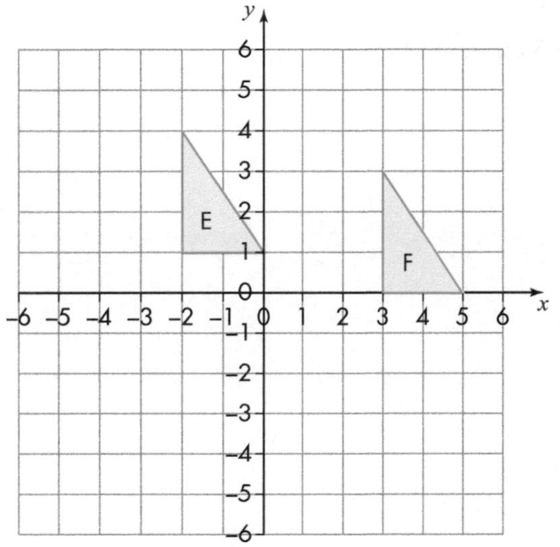

$$\begin{pmatrix} -1 \\ 5 \end{pmatrix} \qquad \begin{pmatrix} -5 \\ 1 \end{pmatrix} \qquad \begin{pmatrix} 5 \\ -1 \end{pmatrix} \qquad \begin{pmatrix} 1 \\ -5 \end{pmatrix}$$

(1)

7 Clive is tiling his kitchen floor. The kitchen is a rectangle measuring 540 cm by 315 cm. He wants to use identical square tiles to cover the floor completely, with no overlap. What is the largest size of square tile that he can use?

_____

_____

_____

_____

(2)

8 Aluminium has a density of 2.7 g/cm³.

A block of aluminium has a mass of 36.45 kg.

a Calculate the volume of the block of aluminium.

_____

_____

_____

(3)

b The block is melted and recast as four identical cubes.

Work out the side length of one of the cubes.

_____

_____

_____

(2)

9 Shade the region of points that satisfy all three of these conditions.

i The points are nearer to AB than BC.

ii The points are nearer to B than C.

iii The points are not further than 5 cm from C. (4)

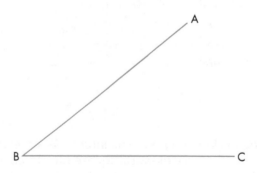

10 $4x + 3y = 27$

$6x - 2y = 8$

Work out the values of x and y.

_____

_____

_____

_____

(3)

11 The diagram shows a regular octagon.

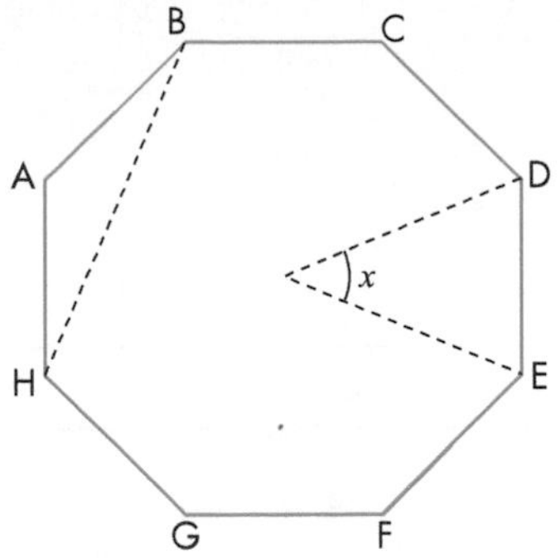

a Work out the size of the angle marked *x*.

_____

(2)

b Work out the size of the interior angle of a regular octagon.

_____

(2)

c Work out the size of angle ABH.

_____

(2)

12 **a** A semicircle of radius 10 cm and a square have the same perimeter.

What is the side length of the square? Give your answer correct to two decimal places.

You must show your working.

_____

_____

_____

(3)

b A circle of diameter 30 cm and a square have the same perimeter.

Which one of them has the greater area?

You must show your working.

_____

_____

_____

_____

_____

_____

_____

_____

_____

(5)

a Work out the value of x.

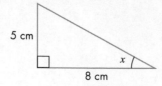

5 cm

8 cm

x

_____

_____

_____

(2)

b Work out the length of the side labelled y.

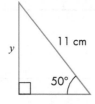

y

11 cm

50°

_____

_____

_____

(2)

14 Solve the equation $x^2 - 8x + 15 = 0$.

_____

_____

_____

(3)

TOTAL MARKS _____ / (64)

Revision paper 3

1 Work out the next term of this quadratic sequence.

2, 8, 17, 29

_____

(2)

2 Factorise fully $12y^2 - 8y$.

_____

(2)

3 Alan's favourite coffee is sold in a 90 g jar for £1.89 and a 300 g jar for £6.20.

a Which jar is better value for money?

You must show your working.

_____

_____

_____

(3)

b Why might Alan **not** buy the jar that is better value for money?

_____

(1)

4 A supermarket recorded the number of minutes 100 shoppers spent in the chocolate aisle before choosing an Easter egg. The table shows the results.

Number of minutes, m	Frequency
$0 < m \leq 1$	20
$1 < m \leq 2$	32
$2 < m \leq 3$	16
$3 < m \leq 4$	12
$4 < m \leq 5$	20

a Calculate an estimate of the mean shopping time.

_____

_____

(4)

b Explain why you cannot work out the exact mean shopping time.

_____

(1)

c Work out the class interval containing the median.

_____

(2)

d The supermarket manager writes a report on the shopping times in the chocolate aisle.

He writes:

'Over 50% of shoppers chose their Easter egg within 2 minutes.'

Is the supermarket manager correct? Give a reason for your answer.

_____

(1)

5 The cost of a luxury private jet is $14 million.

Each year it loses 20% of its value at the start of that year.

Work out its value in 5 years' time.

Give your answer to a sensible degree of accuracy.

_____

_____

_____

(4)

6 Here is a formula.

$v = u + at$

a Work out the value of v when $u = 4$, $a = 5$ and $t = 6$.

_____

(2)

b Rearrange the formula $v = u + at$ to make a the subject.

_____

_____

(2)

7 Farquar buys an old painting for £850. He spends £125 on having it cleaned then sells the painting for £1560. Farquar says that he makes a 50% profit. Is Farquar correct? You must show your working.

_____

_____

_____

_____

(3)

8 Farrouq and Mahmoud are brothers. Each year they share a £1000 gift from their uncle in the ratio of their ages. This year Farrouq is 6 years old and Mahmoud is 2 years old. Show that in four years' time the difference between the amounts they receive will be halved.

_____

_____

_____

_____

_____

(3)

9 A gas supplier uses this formula to work out the total cost of the gas a customer uses.

$C = 0.04G + 30$

where C is the total cost of the gas, in pounds

           G is the number of units of gas used.

a Neal uses 600 units of gas. What is the total cost of the gas he uses?

_____

_____

(2)

b The total cost of the gas Sian uses is £74. How many units of gas does she use?

_____

_____

(2)

10 You are given that $A = 2^3 \times 3^3 \times 5$ and $B = 2 \times 3^4 \times 5^2$.

Write down, as a product of powers of its prime factors:

a the highest common factor (HCF) of A and B

_____

(1)

b the lowest common multiple (LCM) of A and B.

_____

(1)

11 100 university students enrolled for an engineering experience day.

65 of those enrolled were females.

10 females did not turn up to the engineering experience day.

82 university students attended the engineering experience day altogether.

Complete the frequency tree.

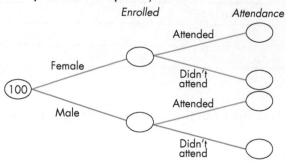

(2)

12 Haritha is tiling his kitchen. The kitchen is a rectangle measuring $3\frac{1}{2}$ m by $5\frac{3}{4}$ m.

Tiles come in packs that cost £15 per pack. Each pack covers an area of 1 m².

Just in case he breaks some tiles, Haritha decides to buy more packs than he needs. He buys an extra 10% of the number of tiles he needs.

How much does Haritha pay for his tiles?

_____

_____

_____

_____

_____

_____

(5)

13 Here are two column vectors.

$$\mathbf{p} = \begin{pmatrix} 6 \\ 4 \end{pmatrix} \qquad \mathbf{q} = \begin{pmatrix} 3 \\ -2 \end{pmatrix}$$

Work out $2\mathbf{p} - 3\mathbf{q}$.

_____

_____

(2)

14 Bob is going to make a raised vegetable plot by putting concrete blocks around a triangular piece of land. The diagram shows the dimensions of the triangle of land.

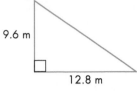

9.6 m

12.8 m

Each concrete block is 40 cm long and costs £1.50 to buy.

How much will it cost Bob to buy the concrete blocks to put around the triangular piece of land?

_____

_____

_____

_____

(6)

15 The diagram shows a hollow triangular prism with no end faces. The surface area of the prism is $(9x + 3)$ cm².

Three of these prisms are joined to make the new prism, as shown. The surface area of the new prism is 50 cm². Work out the value of x.

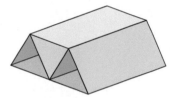

The new shape is a trapezoidal prism.

_____

_____

_____

_____

_____

_____

(5)

16 Complete the table of trigonometric values.

	0°	30°	45°	60°	90°
sin			0.707	0.866	
cos		0.866	0.707		
tan		0.577		1.73	–

(3)

17 The diagram shows a cuboid A and a cone B.

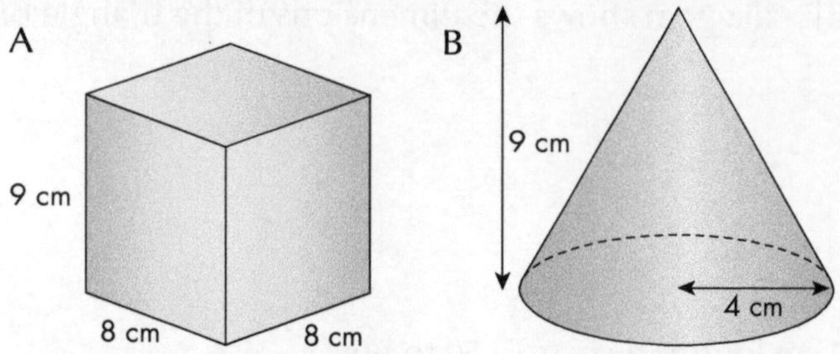

A

B

9 cm

8 cm   8 cm

9 cm

4 cm

Show that the volume of A is less than four times the volume of B.

_____

_____

_____

_____

_____

_____

(5)

TOTAL MARKS _____ / (64)

Notes

Notes

Notes

Notes

Answers

1 Number

1.1 Rounding / Giving an approximate answer

1 a 6   **b** 0.06   **c** 800

2 a 22   **b** 0.87   **c** 57 000

3 a 91.0   **b** 0.0379   **c** 7900

4 a 4000   **b** 7.4   **c** 0.005 56
   d 99.9   **e** 100   **f** 100

5 a 72 800   **b** 36.0   **c** 1870

6 a $70 \times 20 = 1400$ **b** $200 \div 40 = 5$

   c $\dfrac{30 \times 10}{0.5} = 600$ **d** $\dfrac{9 \times 5}{15} = 3$

   e $\dfrac{40\,000}{0.5} = 80\,000$ **f** $\sqrt{81} = 9$

   g $\dfrac{600}{15} = 40$ **h** $\dfrac{600}{0.4} + \dfrac{200}{0.5} = 1900$

7 a 50 or 55   **b** £44 or £47.55

1.2 Prime factors / Lowest common multiples / Highest common factors

1 a $2^2 \times 7$ **b** $2^3 \times 3^2$

2 a 35   **b** 504

3 a 4   **b** 4

4 40 minutes

5 a $2^4 \times 3 \times 5^2$ **b** $2^4 \times 3^3 \times 5^3$

6 a $11^2 \times 23^2$ **b** $11^3 \times 23^3$ **c** $11^7 \times 23^7$

1.3 Indices

1 a 3^5 **b** 10^3 **c** 2^6

2 a a^4 **b** b^2 **c** x^6

3 a 5^4 **b** 7^8 **c** 2^{20}
   d 3^6 **e** 6 (or 6^1)   **f** 8^5
   g y^4 **h** b^8 **i** j^{20}
   j m^4 **k** a **l** 1 (not t^0)
   m 7^2 **n** x^3 **o** x^{-3}
   p d^9

4 a $4a^9$ **b** h^6 **c** $3x^4$
   d $3b$ **e** $2t^3$ **f** a^3

5 $x = 9$

1.4 Fractions

1 a $\dfrac{25}{28}$ **b** $\dfrac{38}{45}$ **c** $\dfrac{7}{30}$
   d $\dfrac{5}{36}$

2 a $4\frac{14}{15}$ **b** $1\frac{19}{40}$ **c** $6\frac{11}{12}$
   d $4\frac{5}{12}$ **e** $\dfrac{3}{8}$ **f** $\dfrac{2}{3}$
   g $4\frac{3}{8}$ **h** 8 **i** $10\frac{1}{2}$
   j $33\frac{3}{5}$ **k** $\dfrac{3}{4}$ **l** $1\frac{1}{3}$
   m $10\frac{6}{25}$ **n** $\dfrac{1}{4}$

3 $7\frac{3}{20}$ m^2

4 15 strides

5 a $6\frac{19}{40}$ **b** $5\frac{3}{8}$

6 a $1\frac{2}{3}$ **b** $1\frac{7}{9}$

1.5 Percentage increase and decrease

1 £280

2 £2.80

3 39.6 m

4 3.96 m

5 4%

6 28.04%

7 a 346.5 cm^2
   b Smaller. $1 \times 1.1 \times 0.9 = 0.99$

8 £355.50

9 4.4π

1.6 One quantity as a percentage of another

1 a 20%   **b** 25%   **c** 53.3%
   d 10%   **e** 37.5%   **f** 8.3%

2 English = 60%, history = 62.2% so Jodie is better at history than English.

3 48.4%

4 21.1%

5 150%

6 0.6%

7 50%

1.7 Compound interest

1 $2000, invested for 3 years, at a rate of 5% per year.

2 £1192.52

3 Approximately 540 000

4 £10 555

5 Approximately 600 000

6 a 4.07 m   **b** 13 years

7 5 years

8 £480

1.8 Basic powers and roots

1 16, 25, 36, 49, 64, 81, 100, 121, 144, 169, 196, 225

2 27, 64, 125

3 a 10   **b** 12   **c** 4   **d** 1
   e 10   **f** 12   **g** 3

4 4 and −4

5 −10 × −10 = +100

6 a 26   **b** 302.8   **c** 3.1
   d 0.3   **e** 0.008   **f** 16

7 a 2   **b** 6

8 a 29   **b** 117   **c** 7

9 a 0.7   **b** 1.1   **c** 0.2

1.9 Reciprocals

1 a i $\frac{1}{2}$ **ii** 0.5   **b i** $\frac{1}{5}$ **ii** 0.2

   c i $\frac{1}{10}$ **ii** 0.1   **d i** $\frac{1}{100}$ **ii** 0.01

2 Decimal becomes smaller.

3 a 4   **b** 0.4   **c** 0.04   **d** 40

4 a $1\frac{2}{7}$ **b** $\frac{9}{16}$ **c** $\frac{9}{25}$ **d** $\frac{9}{34}$

5 a 2.5   **b** 0.4   **c** 1   **d** 1
   e yes

6 For example, the reciprocal of 0.1 is 10.

7 $\frac{1}{8}$

1.10 Standard index form

1 6.023×10^{23}

2 1.37×10^{18} m³

3 2×10^{-8} m

4 3.3×10^{-25} g

5 a 10 000   **b** 120 000   **c** 0.000 012 3
   d 0.1234

6 a 6.2×10^{3} **b** 5.8×10^{3} **c** 1.2×10^{6}
   d 3×10^{1}

7 1.53×10^{8}

8 2×10^{0} kg

9 135 kg

1.11 Surds

1 a $\sqrt{15}$ **b** $2\sqrt{15}$

2 a 5   **b** 6   **c** 20
   d 12   **e** 10   **f** 3

3 a $2\sqrt{3}$ **b** $4\sqrt{5}$

4 a 42   **b** 24   **c** $8\sqrt{6}$
   d $6\sqrt{15}$ **e** $18\sqrt{6}$ **f** $4\sqrt{5}$
   g 10   **h** $13\sqrt{2}$ **I** $3\sqrt{3}$

2 Algebra

2.1 Factorising

1 a $6(a + 2)$ **b** $4(a + 2b)$ **c** $2(2x + 3y)$

  d $2(4t - 3p)$ **e** $2a(b + 3c)$ **f** $5m(n - p)$

  g $p(p + 5)$ **h** $h(7 - h)$ **i** $x(3x + 2)$

2 a $3t(t - p)$ **b** $3x(2x + 3y)$ **c** $4a(3a - 2b)$

  d $4bc(b + 2)$ **e** $2b(4ac - 3ed)$ **f** $2ab(1 + 2a)$

  g $2(2x^2 + 3x + 4y)$ **h** $3m(2p + 3b + t)$

  i $2cd(4d - 1 - 2c - 6cd)$

3 a length $= 4x + 3$ **b** length $= 3 - 2p$

4 length $= t + 4$

5 a $n(n - 1)$

  b If n is odd then $n - 1$ is even and if n is even then $n - 1$ is odd.

    odd × even = even

6 $y(x + \frac{1}{2}z)$

7 a $(x + 1)(x + 2)$ **b** $(x + 3)(x + 3)$ **c** $(x - 2)(x + 3)$

8 a $(x + 3)(x - 3)$ **b** $(x + 10)(x - 10)$
  c $(x + 7)(x - 7)$ **d** $(x + 1)(x - 1)$

2.2 Brackets

1 a $5a + 10$ **b** $20 + 5x$ **c** $5x - 5y$
  d $x^2 + x$ **e** $7x - x^2$ **f** $x^2 - xy$
  g $15a + 5a^2$ **h** $15a^2 + 5ab$ **i** $5a^3 - 15a^2b$

2 a $5x + 12$ **b** $14x + 13y$ **c** $3x^2 + 2x$
  d $7x^2 + 7x$ **e** $2a^2 + 6ab$ **f** $6x^2 + 5xy + 6y^2$
  g $23a^2 + 14a$ **h** $16p^2q^2 - 10p^2r - 2q^2r$

3 a $y(x + 1) + x(y + 1)$ **b** $2xy + x + y$

4 a $4(x + 1) + 6(x + 2)$ **b** $2(3x + 1) - 3(x - 4)$

    $= 4x + 4 + 6x + 12$ $= 6x + 2 - 3x + 12$

    $= 10x + 16$ $= 3x + 14$

    $= 2(5x + 8)$ $= 3x + 15 - 1$

                        $= 3(x + 5) - 1$

2.3 Solving linear equations

1 a $x = 2$ **b** $x = \frac{1}{2}$
  c $x = 9$ **d** $x = 5$

2 a $x = -3$ **b** $x = 3.5$ **c** $x = 4$
  d $x = 1$ **e** $x = 0.2$

3 a $x = 2.5$ **b** $x = 1.5$

2.4 Solving quadratic equations

1 $x = -1, x = -2$

2 $x = -1, x = -3$

3 $x = -3$

4 $x = 3$

5 $x = 2, x = -3$

6 $x = 4, x = -2$

7 $x = 3, x = -3$

8 $x = 12, x = -12$

2.5 Set up and solve linear equations

1 a $10x = 180$ **b** $x = 18$ **c** 36°, 36° and 108°

2 a $\frac{n}{2} + 4 = n + 1$ **b** $n = 6$

3 a $5(x - 2) = 3(x + 4)$ **b** $x = 11$

4 33 years old

5 12 years old

6 6

7 a $6(2x - 1) = 8(x + 5)$ **b** $x = 11.5$

8 $x = 0.6$

9 £2.15

2.6 Rearranging (changing the subject of) formulae

1 a $a = x - 6$ **b** $a = y + 6$ **c** $a = 6 - z$

2 a $b = \frac{x - 6}{4}$ **b** $b = \frac{y + 3}{5}$ **c** $b = \frac{6 - z}{2}$

3 a $R = \frac{V}{I}$ **b** $b = \frac{P}{4}$ **c** $b = \frac{2A}{h}$

  d $c = y - mx$ **e** $m = \frac{y - c}{x}$ **f** $C = \frac{5(F - 32)}{9}$

4 a $r = \sqrt{\dfrac{A}{\pi}}$ **b** $r = \sqrt{\dfrac{V}{\pi h}}$ **c** $r = \sqrt[3]{\dfrac{3V}{4\pi}}$

d $r = \dfrac{9}{5}$ or 1.8 **e** $r = \dfrac{1}{P}$ **f** $r = \dfrac{2}{3Q}$

2.7 The nth term

1 a even numbers **b** odd numbers
  c square numbers **d** Fibonacci

2 a 7, 12, 17, 22 **b** 502

3 a 1, 3, 6, 10 **b** 5050

4 a 2, 6, 12, 20 **b** 10 100

5 a 0, 5, 14, 27 **b** 19 899

6 a $5n$ **b** $2n$ **c** $50n$ **d** $20n$

7 a $5n + 1$ **b** $2n + 1$ **c** $4n - 1$
  d $5n - 4$ **e** $3n - 7$ **f** $10n - 90$

8 a $13 - 3n$ **b** $24 - 4n$ **c** $107 - 10n$
  d $-5n$ **e** $3 - 3n$ **f** $11 - 10n$

9 a $\dfrac{2n+1}{5n-1}$ **b** $\dfrac{n}{3n-1}$ **c** $\dfrac{4n-1}{107-10n}$

  d $\dfrac{3-4n}{n+5}$

10 $4n - 2$

11 a $3n + 2$ **b** 50 tables

12 a 2^n **b** 10^n

2.8 Inequalities

1 a $x < 5$ **b** $x \geqslant 14$ **c** $x \leqslant 7$
  d $x < 4$ **e** $x \geqslant 1$ **f** $x \leqslant -2$
  g $x > 30$ **h** $x \geqslant 8$ **i** $x < -2$

2 a $x = 5$ **b** $x = 13$ **c** $x = -5$
  d $x = 4$ **e** $x = -6$ **f** $x = 2$

3 a $x = 8$ **b** $x = 13$ **c** $x = 9$ **d** $x = 11$

4 a $x \geqslant 1$ **b** $x < 3$ **c** $0 < x \leqslant 4$ **d** $-3 \leqslant x \leqslant 1$

5 a 1, 2 **b** 1, 2 **c** 1

6 a

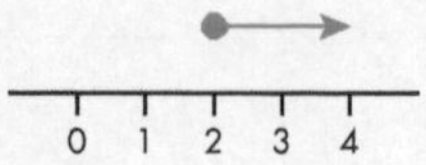

(number line: filled circle at 2, arrow right; scale 0 1 2 3 4)

b

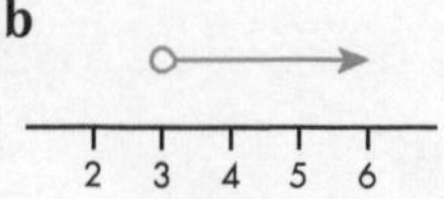

(number line: open circle at 3, arrow right; scale 2 3 4 5 6)

c

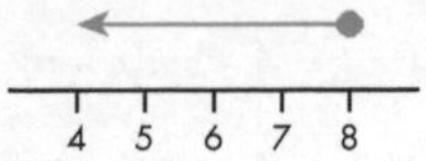

(number line: filled circle at 7, arrow left; scale 4 5 6 7 8)

d

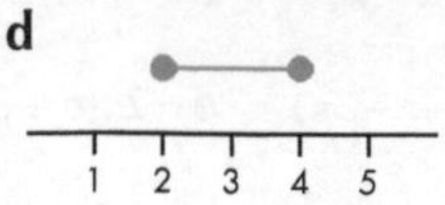

(number line: filled circle at 1 to filled circle at 4; scale 1 2 3 4 5)

e

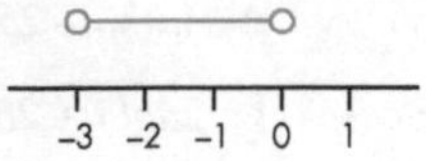

(number line: open circle at −2 to open circle at 0; scale −3 −2 −1 0 1)

f

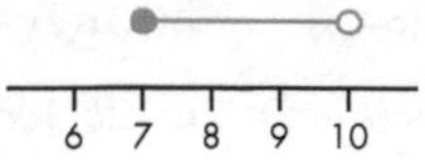

(number line: filled circle at 7 to open circle at 9; scale 6 7 8 9 10)

7 $x \leqslant 1.5$

(number line: filled circle at 1.5, arrow left; scale 0 0.5 1 1.5 2)

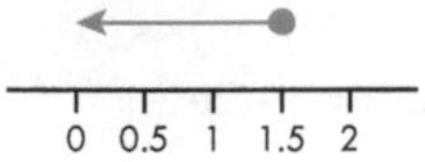

8 $0 \leqslant x < 4$

2.9 Real-life graphs

1 a i 12:00 **ii** 15:00 **b** 160 miles
  c i 20 mph **ii** 40 mph

2 a A = 4, B is unmatched, C = 1, D = 5, E = 3, F = 2

  b

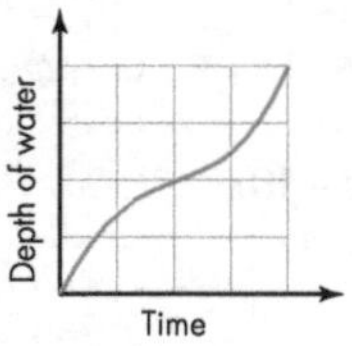

3 a A to B: 40 km/h; B to C: 5 km/h; C to D: 0 km/h; D to E: 30 km/h
  b The steepest section is A to B.

4 a 6 km/h **b** 0.6 m/minute
  c 0.8 km/h **d** 1.4 km/minute

5 Rob keeps a steady pace throughout to win the race. Darren sets off more quickly, but slows down and is overtaken. He then speeds up again but can't catch Rob.

2.10 Gradient and intercept

1 A: $\dfrac{1}{2}$, B: 1, C: 2, D: 2, E: −2, F: $-\dfrac{1}{2}$

2 a 4 **b** 1 **c** $-\dfrac{1}{2}$ **d** −2

3 a 4 **b** 3

4 a D **b** A and E, B and C, F and G, H and I **c** I

5 a $y = x + 1$ **b** $y = 2x + 3$ **c** $y = \dfrac{1}{2}x - 4$

2.11 Drawing linear graphs

1

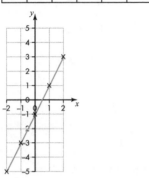

2 a

x	−2	−1	0	1	2
y	−5	−3	−1	1	3

b

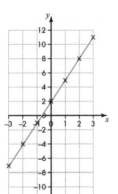

c $x = 0.5$

3 a   **b** $x = -2$

4

a $y = 2x + 2$
c $y = x + 2$
b $y = -\frac{1}{2}x + 2$
d $y = 5 - 2x$

2.12 Drawing quadratic graphs

1 a

x	−4	−3	−2	−1	0	1	2	3
y	18	11	6	3	2	3	6	11

b

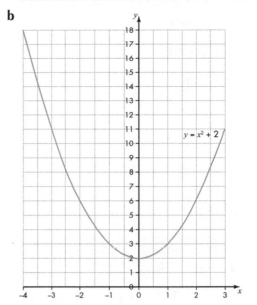

$y = x^2 + 2$

c $y = 4.25$

2 a

x	−2	−1	0	1	2	3
y	15	5	−1	−3	−1	5

b

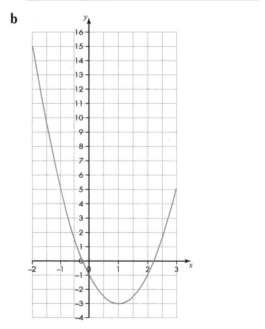

c **i** Look for points where the curve crosses the *x*-axis.

   ii 2.22

2.13 Recognising shapes of graphs

1 $y = x^2 + 1$ is graph G.

2 $y = 2x^2 + 1$ is graph I.

3 $y = x^2 - 1$ is graph B.

4 $y = x^2 + 2x$ is graph E.

5 $y = 2x + 1$ is graph A.

6 $y = x^3 + 1$ is graph H.

7 $y = -x^3 + 1$ is graph F.

8 $y = \frac{1}{2}x^2 + 2x + 1$ is graph C.

9 $y = \frac{1}{x}$ is graph D.

2.14 Simultaneous equations

1 a $x = 2, y = 5$ **b** $x = 2, y = 3$

2 a $x = 2, y = 4$ **b** $x = 2, y = 3$ **c** $x = 5, y = 3$

3 120

3 Ratio, proportion and rates of change

3.1 Sharing an amount in a given ratio

1 20, 30

2 160 g, 240 g

3 £27, £63

4 10 m, 990 m

5 20 ml , 30 ml, 50 ml

6 6.75 kg, 5.625 kg, 1.125 kg

7 500 kg cement, 1000 kg sand, 2000 kg gravel

8 a Aaron £1188, Beth £1782, Charlie £2970
b £90

9 40°

3.2 Using ratio

1 4 male teachers

2 60 teachers

3 38 staff

4 a 315 **b** 630

5 20 litres lemonade, 0.5 litres ginger

6 £69.75

7 1 : 2

3.3 Direct and indirect proportion

1 a $T = 18$ **b** $P = 1\frac{1}{2}$

2 a $R = \frac{1}{2}$ **b** $S = \frac{1}{3}$

3 a $A = 75$ **b** $D = 6$

4 a D **b** A **c** B

4 Geometry and measures

4.1 Circles – circumference

1 a 31.4 cm **b** 11.3 mm **c** 596.9 m
d 62.8 cm **e** 22.6 mm **f** 1193.8 m

2 a 175.9 cm **b** 284 **c** 2 512 374

3 a 20π mm **b** $1.4 \times 10^2\pi$ km **c** 7.6π m

4 113 097 cm ÷ 125.7 cm = 899 revolutions

5 a 25.7 cm **b** 21.4 cm

6 a $(5\pi + 20)$ cm **b** $(10\pi + 30)$ cm

7 95.5 cm

8 0.16 m

9 99.4 cm

4.2 Circles – area

1 a 78.5 cm² **b** 10.2 mm² **c** 28 352.9 m²
d 314.2 cm² **e** 40.7 mm² **f** 113 411.5 m²

2 a 100π mm² **b** $4.9 \times 10^{11}\pi$ km² **c** 14.44π m²

3 a 78.54 cm² **b** 257.08 cm²

4 a 21.46 cm² **b** 85.84 cm² **c** 23.18 cm²

5 a 128π cm² **b** 64π cm²
c 32π cm² **d** 16π cm²

4.3 Prisms and 3D shapes – surface area

1 190 cm^2

2 84 cm^2

3 211.2 cm^2

4 240 cm^2

5 664 cm^2

6 296 cm^2

7 314.2 cm^2

8 1206.4 cm^2

9 10

4.4 Prisms and 3D shapes – volume

1 150 cm^3

2 261 cm^3

3 192 cm^3

4 288 cm^3

5 1100 cm^3

6 37 699 cm^3

7 1590.43 cm^3

8 $2 \times 10 \times 3 \times 5 = \frac{1}{2} \times 4 \times 5 \times 30$

  300 = 300 ✓

9 523.6 cm^3

10 300 cm^3

4.5 Density and pressure

1 a 0.8 g/cm^3 **b** 45 cm^3 **c** 189 g

2 a 400 N   **b** 0.5 N/cm^2 **c** 40 cm^2

3 33 180 kg

4 0.9 N/cm^2

5 86.4 g

4.6 Similar shapes

1 No, because 25 : 20 ≠ 19 : 14

2 a $x = 8.4$ cm   **b** $y = 7.5$ cm   **c** $z = 92°$

3 No. 10 : 30 ≠ 6 : 20 or 8 : 24 ≠ 6 : 20

4 a ∠ABC = ∠EDC (alternate angles), ∠BAC = ∠DEC (alternate angles), ∠ACB = ∠ECD (vertically opposite angles)

  b i $x = 27$ cm   **ii** $y = 14.5$ cm

5 $x = 13.2$ cm, $y = 4.8$ cm

6 31.5 m

7 40°

4.7 Congruent triangles

1 a Yes, SSS
  b No, 6 cm in the wrong position to be congruent.
  c Yes, ASA (180° − 60° − 70° = 50°)
  d Yes, RHS

2 ABE is congruent to ADE, BCE is congruent to CDE.

3 PQT is congruent to RST, QRT is congruent to PST.

4.8 Trigonometry

1 a 30°   **b** 8.5 m   **c** 8 cm

2 65.1°

3 21.1 km

4 32.1 cm^2

4.9 Arcs and sectors

1 a 20.9 cm   **b** 8.38 cm   **c** 26.2 cm

2 a 6π cm^2 **b** 27π cm^2 **c** 4.8π cm^2

3 a 88.36 m^2 **b** $10 + 11.25\pi$ m

4.10 Pythagoras' theorem

1 a 13   **b** 7.1   **c** 9.9

2 a 6   **b** 6.6   **c** 7.2

3 14.1 cm

4 131.4 m

5 3.3 m

6 5.1 cm

7 a 5 units   **b** 8 units

8 16.40

4.11 Regular polygons

1 a 108°   **b** 72°

2 A hexagon can be divided into 4 triangles. The angle sum of a triangle is 180° and 4 × 180° = 720°.

3 8

4 External angles = 180° – 160° = 20° so number of sides = 360 ÷ 20 = 18

5 $a = 120°$, $b = 30°$, $c = 90°$

6 70°

4.12 Translation

1 a 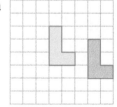   **b**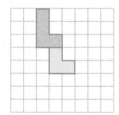

2 a 1 square right, 4 squares up
  b 4 squares left, 3 squares up
  c 5 squares left, 1 square down
  d 1 square left, 4 squares down

3 a $\begin{pmatrix} 2 \\ -3 \end{pmatrix}$ **b** $\begin{pmatrix} -4 \\ 4 \end{pmatrix}$ **c** $\begin{pmatrix} -4 \\ -4 \end{pmatrix}$

  d $\begin{pmatrix} -2 \\ 3 \end{pmatrix}$ **e** $\begin{pmatrix} 4 \\ 0 \end{pmatrix}$ **f** $\begin{pmatrix} 0 \\ 4 \end{pmatrix}$

4.13 More vectors

1 $\begin{pmatrix} 6 \\ 2 \end{pmatrix}$

2 a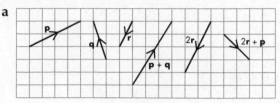

  b i $\begin{pmatrix} 3 \\ 0 \end{pmatrix}$ **ii** $\begin{pmatrix} -2 \\ 1 \end{pmatrix}$ **iii** $\begin{pmatrix} 5 \\ -1 \end{pmatrix}$ **iv** $\begin{pmatrix} 0 \\ 5 \end{pmatrix}$

  v $\begin{pmatrix} 8 \\ 4 \end{pmatrix}$ **vi** $\begin{pmatrix} -3 \\ 9 \end{pmatrix}$ **vii** $\begin{pmatrix} 1 \\ 2 \end{pmatrix}$ **viii** $\begin{pmatrix} -2 \\ 11 \end{pmatrix}$

4.14 Rotation

1 a 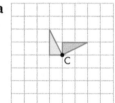   **b**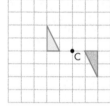

2 a, b, c

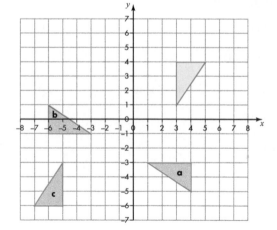

3 a

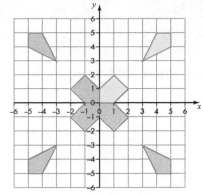

b

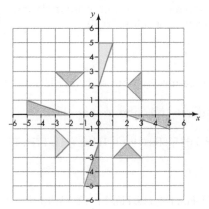

4.15 Reflection

1

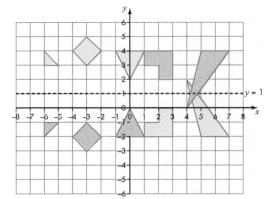

2

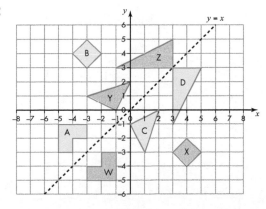

3 a Reflection in the line $x = -3$
 b Reflection in the line $y = -1$
 c Reflection in the line $y = -x$
 d Reflection in the line $y = x$
 e Reflection in the line $y = x$

4.16 Enlargement

1

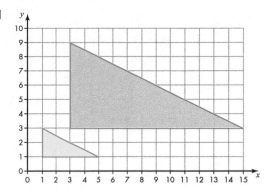

2

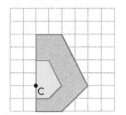

3 a

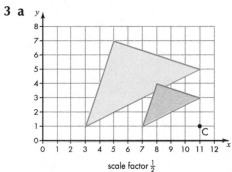

scale factor $\frac{1}{2}$

b

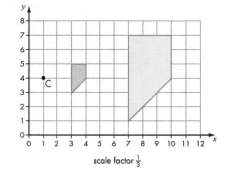

scale factor $\frac{1}{3}$

c

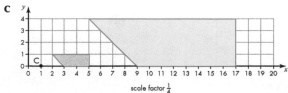

scale factor $\frac{1}{4}$

4.17 Constructions

Check that all constructions are accurate and that construction lines are shown.

4.18 Loci

1

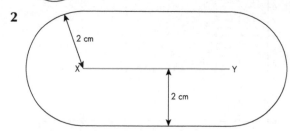

2

3

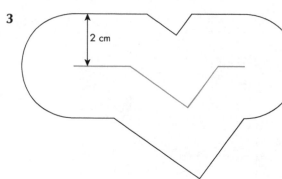

4

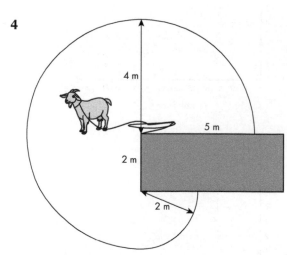

5

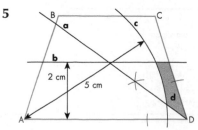

5 Probability

5.1 Basic probability

1 a 0.3, 0.12, 0.19, 0.15, 0.184, 0.163

  b $\frac{1}{6}$

  c 1000

2 500

3 a 100   **b** 200   **c** 250   **d** 0

4 Janet, as she has carried out more trials and her frequencies are all close to 50.

5 a $\frac{1}{2}$ **b** $\frac{1}{2}$

  c A card cannot be both red and black.

  d A card must be either red or black.

6 a HHH, HHT, HTH, HTT, THH, THT, TTH, TTT

  b $\frac{1}{8}$ **c** $\frac{3}{8}$

7 a H1, H2, H3, H4, H5, H6, T1, T2, T3, T4, T5, T6

  b $\frac{1}{12}$

8 $\frac{1}{36}$

9 a

	1	2	3	4
1	2	3	4	5
2	3	4	5	6
3	4	5	6	7
4	5	6	7	8

  b $\frac{3}{16}$

10 $\frac{1}{8}$

11 a 0.27   **b** 850   **c** 357

12 a

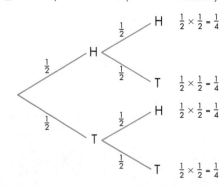

b i $\frac{1}{4}$ **ii** $\frac{1}{4}$ **iii** $\frac{1}{2}$ **iv** $\frac{3}{4}$

13 a

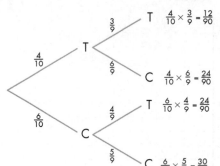

Probability

$\frac{4}{10} \times \frac{3}{9} = \frac{12}{90}$

$\frac{4}{10} \times \frac{6}{9} = \frac{24}{90}$

$\frac{6}{10} \times \frac{4}{9} = \frac{24}{90}$

$\frac{6}{10} \times \frac{5}{9} = \frac{30}{90}$

b $\frac{12}{90}$ or $\frac{2}{15}$ **c** $\frac{60}{90}$ or $\frac{2}{3}$ **d** $\frac{30}{90}$ or $\frac{1}{3}$

5.2 Frequency trees

1

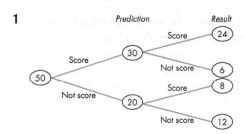

2 a

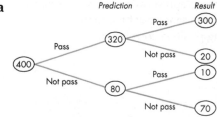

b 22.5%

5.3 Venn diagrams

1

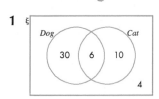

2 a

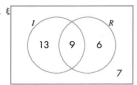

b $\frac{7}{35}$ or $\frac{1}{5}$ **c** $\frac{28}{35}$ or $\frac{4}{5}$

3 a 41 **b** $\frac{23}{41}$ **c** $\frac{18}{41}$

d $\frac{9}{41}$ **e** $\frac{31}{41}$ **f** $\frac{8}{41}$

4 a

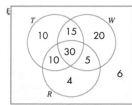

b i $\frac{6}{100}$ or 0.06 **ii** $\frac{20}{100}$ or 0.2

6 Statistics

6.1 Mean, median, mode and range

1 a £29 000 **b** £18 000 **c** £21 000 **d** £21 500

e £29 000 **f** £20 000 **g** £23 000 **h** £23 500

2 a 3 **b** 2, 5 **c** 4 **d** 3.5

3 a 6 **b** 6 **c** 6 **d** 5.7

4 a 124 **b** 2.54

5 a $5 < x \leqslant 10$ **b** 9.4

6 a $20 < x \leqslant 30$ **b** 27
   c You do not know the highest or lowest values.

7 6.8

8 84 kg

9 78.8 kg

10 2.35

6.2 Bar charts

1

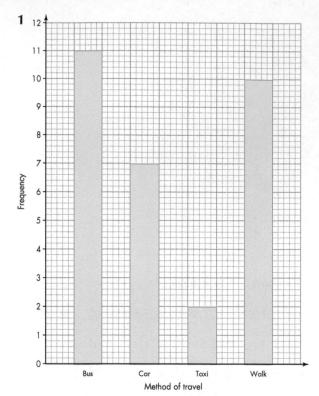

Method of travel

2 a No. 9 were sold Monday and 12 on Friday.

b Any two mistakes, for example:

No label for vertical axis. Bar chart does not start at zero. The bar chart starts at 6 but there is no zigzag line. The gaps between the bars are not the same.

6.3 Pie charts

a 25%

b Student's comparison, for example, the number of people that did not own a dog is the same as the number of people that do own at least one dog.

c $\frac{60}{360}$ or $\frac{1}{6}$

d 2400

6.4 Correlation

1 a

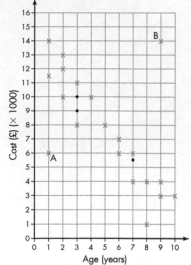

Age (years)

b Yes, the graph shows negative correlation.

c **i** A cheaper make/model of car

ii A more expensive make/model of car

d The trend cannot continue indefinitely as the car would be worth a negative amount. Eventually the car will be worth a minimum or 'scrap' value.

2 a Yes, the graph shows positive correlation.

b Low attendance but high mark

c Strong positive correlation

d

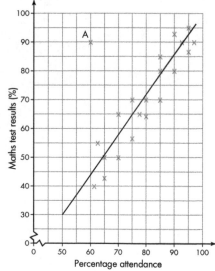

Percentage attendance

e **i** 75–82% **ii** 70–75%

f This value lies outside the range of the given data.

3 a, b

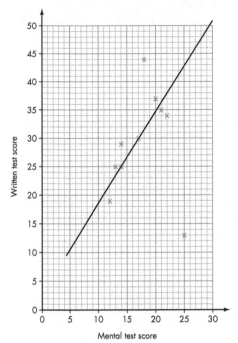

c 17–19

d Dom – position lies well below line of best fit.

6.5 Time series graphs

1 a

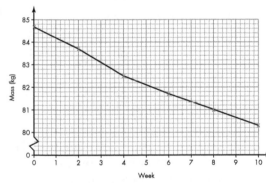

b 83.1 kg
c Between weeks 2 and 4
d The trend is downward.
e No. Reasons could include that the loss in mass is not the same in each two-week period, you do not know if Neil sticks to his diet, he might have reached his target, etc.

2 a

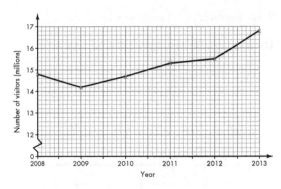

b Student's answer and reason, e.g. 17.2 million as average increase of 0.4 million.
c 2012 to 20134
d Increasing. Check student's reason.
e No, there are too many unknowns in the future for prediction to be possible.

Revision paper 1

1 a $\dfrac{100}{5} = 20$ **b** $\dfrac{450}{10} = 45$

2 12

3 $3n + 1$

4 a $2(n + 4)$ double any number and get an even number

  b 9th term   **c** $\dfrac{4n - 3}{38 - 3n}$

5 $a < 5$

6 $2^2 \times 3^3 \times 5$

7 2008: $1000 \times £10 = £10\,000$

2009: $1200 \times £8 = £9\,600$

No, the florist takes less money in 2009.

OR $1.2 \times 0.8 = 0.96$, 96% is less so the florist takes less money

8 a, c, d

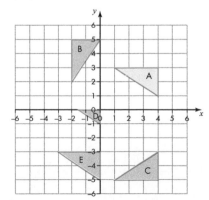

b $y = -1$

9 For example, $n = 1$ gives $n^2 + 2 = 3$.

10 a 30 cm, 31 cm, 32 cm, 33 cm, 34 cm

b

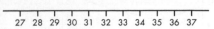

27 28 29 30 31 32 33 34 35 36 37

11 a 5

b No, $6^{15} \div 6^5 = 6^{10}$. The rule is to subtract the indices.

12 a

x	−3	−2	−1	0	1	2	3
y	17	10	5	2	1	2	5

b

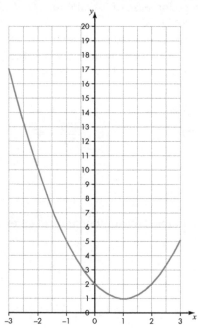

c $y = 3.25$

(accept $y = 3$ to 3.5)

d $x = -0.75$ and $x = 2.75$

13 a i

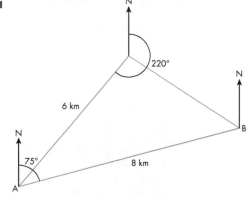

ii approx 4.6 (±0.2) km on a bearing of 303°(±5°)

b

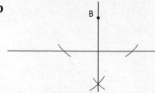

14 a Because $\sqrt{9} = 3$ **b** $\sqrt{12} = 2\sqrt{3}$ **c** $\sqrt{3}$

15 a 972 or 1200 cm²

b Underestimate. Both numbers have been rounded down. Used π as 3 (not 3.142…) and radius as 9 cm (not 9.24 cm) or Overestimate, as radius has been rounded up to 10 for an easier calculation.

Revision paper 2

1 £1560

2 a, c

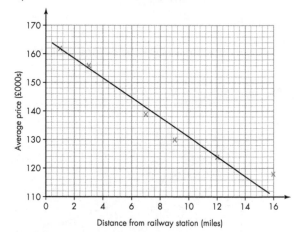

b Negative correlation

d Approximately 4.5 miles (Answer may vary slightly depending on line of best fit.)

e This distance lies outside the given information.

3 a $x = 2.7$ **b** $3x^2 - 4x$

c $9d + 14$ **d** $x^2 - 4x - 12$

4 Yes: percentage increase is 5% and $546\,000 \times 1.05\% = 696\,850 \approx 700\,000$

5 a $\dfrac{37}{50}$

b Don't know the individual values spent.

c 360

6 $\begin{pmatrix} 5 \\ -1 \end{pmatrix}$

7 45 cm

8 a 13 500 cm³ [or 0.0135 m³]
  b 15 cm

9 **iii** circle, radius 5 cm, centred on C

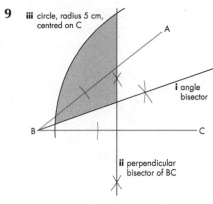

10 $x = 3, y = 5$

11 a 45° **b** 135° **c** 22.5°

12 a Perimeter of semicircle = 51.415 cm, side length = 12.85 cm
  b Circumference = 94.247 cm, side length = 23.56 cm.
  Area of circle = 706.86 cm², area of square = 555.17 cm². Circle.

13 a 32° **b** 8.426 cm

14 $x = 3, x = 5$

Revision paper 3

1 44

2 $4y(3y - 2)$

3 a 300 g jar (is 2.067p/g, 90 g jar is 2.1p/g)
  b Student's reason, e.g. might not drink much coffee, might not want to spend so much.

4 a 2.3 minutes (or 2 minutes 18 seconds)
  b You don't have each shopper's individual time.
  c $1 < m \leq 2$
  d Yes, 52% chose in less than 2 minutes.

5 $4.6 million

6 a 34

  b $a = \dfrac{v - u}{t}$

7 No: 1560 − 975 = 585 and 585 ÷ 975 × 100 = 60%

8 Ratio = 3 : 1 Farrouq receives £750, Mahmoud receives £250, difference = £500

  In 4 years' time ratio is 5 : 3

  Farrouq receives £625, Mahmoud receives £375, difference = £250

9 a £54 **b** 1100 units

10 a $2 \times 3^3 \times 5$ **b** $2^3 \times 3^4 \times 5^2$

11

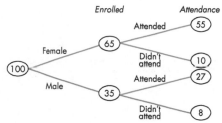

12 23 × £15 = £345 or 22 packs × £15 = £330 [as rounding down is reasonable]

13 $\begin{pmatrix} 3 \\ 14 \end{pmatrix}$

14 Hypotenuse length = 16 m

  Total length = 38.4 m ÷ 0.4 = 96 blocks
  96 × £1.50 = £144

15 One face = $3x + 1, x = 3$ cm

16

	0°	30°	45°	60°	90°
sin	0	0.5	0.707	0.866	1
cos	1	0.866	0.707	0.5	0
tan	0	0.577	1	1.73	–

17 A = 576 cm³, B = 150.796 cm³,
  4B = 603.185 cm³, 576 < 603